Bru

www.pocketessentials.com

Bruce Springsteen

Peter Basham

www.pocketessentials.com

This edition published in February 2005 by Pocket Essentials
P.O. Box 394, Harpenden, Herts, AL5 1XJ
www.pocketessentials.com

Distributed in the USA by Trafalgar Square Publishing, P.O. Box 257, Howe Hill
Road, North Pomfret, Vermont 05053

A CIP catalogue record for this book is available from the British Library.

ISBN 1 903047 97 8

Typeset by Avocet, Typeset, Chilton, Aylesbury, Bucks
Printed and bound in Great Britain by Cox & Wyman, Reading

Acknowledgements

Thanks to my family and friends. Special thanks to Ed for expert advice and to Florence for amazing patience.

Contents

Introduction

Bruce Springsteen is not a musical pioneer, but he is a great artist. He has survived youthful hype – he appeared simultaneously on the covers of *Time* (with the story 'Rock's New Sensation') and *Newsweek* ('Making of a Rock star') when just twenty-six years old. At his first peak of popularity he endured a protracted legal battle against his then manager, the aggressive, but undeniably resourceful, Mike Appel. Albums such as *Nebraska*, *Tunnel Of Love* and *The Ghost Of Tom Joad* have seen Springsteen follow his muse rather than the obvious commercial path that his writing could easily have seen him mine, and yet time and again he has resurfaced at the very top, against expectation or industry trend. Ultimately, he has weathered the fickle changes in taste from generation to generation, still remains capable of selling millions of records, and is now a hugely respected old-timer who has confounded his critics by remaining decidedly down-to-earth in nature and well-liked by those with whom he has worked.

What his career has shown is that Bruce Springsteen has an uncanny ability to write narratives that cover any subject that connects to, or interests him. That he is able to do this with a clarity and directness, particularly after the adrenalin rushes of his first two records, distinguishes him from both contemporaries and those predecessors who so influenced him. Greil Marcus acknowledges "it's just amazing how much he can do in just two or three lines... you know exactly where you are and you can follow the story". It is Bruce's dedication to a largely narrative and direct style of songwriting, as opposed to simple boy-meets-girl or girl-leaves-boy or the abstract imagery of other artists, that separates him and gives his work a vivid, often widescreen cinematic feel. With this directness of storytelling and a recurring working-class man versus hard-nosed authority theme, it is not surprising to find that Bruce has drawn from the cinema world. An artist who collects phrases and lines for potential lyrics, Bruce has notched up a number of tracks that borrow film titles. 'Thunder Road' was previously a Robert Mitchum boot-legging/gangland film and 'Badlands' shares the title of Terrence Malick's movie account of the Starkweather murder spree, a story that Bruce would actually describe years later on the title track of his *Nebraska* album. The brooding and regretful 'Point Blank' and the paranoid *Born In The U.S.A.* outtake 'Murder Incorporated' also hark back to classic film noir, a world where typically a good man at heart is forced to struggle against corruption and injustice just to get by, emerging, if at all, with an ambiguous sense of survival.

Bruce Springsteen's own life story has been one of outstanding success, musical integrity and resilience, notching up hit albums in each decade of his professional recording career. From the youthful drive of 1975's *Born To Run*, through to his first U.S. number one with 1980's *The River*, and on to the stately 'comeback' of 2002, *The Rising*, Bruce has remained at the very top of his profession. For all his successes, however, critics continually make play of Springsteen for singing his songs full of desperate working-class lives while he himself is performing in the wealthy arena of the world's huge, bland stadiums. A simplistic view is that Springsteen has exploited themes of blue-collar life whilst attaining a great personal wealth. However, aside from the fact that Bruce's early life was not one of great comfort or stability and he knew the hardships of working life through his father, Bruce has attained his wealth through hard work that should be heralded for the inspiration it offers to others – not to become megastars as he has, but to make something of themselves according to their own talents. He personifies his lyric (dramatically adapted from an Elvis Presley recording) urging that we should "Follow That Dream".

Another criticism of Bruce is that he frequently, and therefore unimaginatively uses cars as props in his work. Just a cursory glance at Springsteen's song titles, art work and lyrics will indeed reveal his considerable lyrical use of the automobile. For Bruce, however, cars and roads are potent vehicles, or rather metaphors, for so much of the deeper significance that he is looking to address. They provide a perceived route of escape for the youths in 'Thunder Road', through to *The Rising* album where cars are no longer racing around, but "snakin' slow through town", embodying the mourning of a community. Even here, however, there is a hope that one-day strength will be found "further on up the road". Elsewhere – and there are a lot of examples! – cars are symbols of oppression in 'Seeds', lust in 'Pink Cadillac' and temporary release in 'Racing In The Street'. 'Stolen Car' depicts the dramatic loss of purpose in a relationship, 'Used Cars' finds their value as social status symbols and the loneliness of driving alone runs through 'Valentine's Day'. Cars and huge open roads are a classic and very American picture and, rather than being lazily used by Springsteen, they give a sense of consistency to his narratives. Through all their various symbolic purposes, the solid form of this everyday utility is an unremarkable presence that the singer chooses to remark upon and draws moods from. Away from this seriousness, Bruce is certainly aware of the view of him as car-obsessed and is prepared to admit to his regular use of the motif with humour. At a Woody Guthrie tribute concert in 1996 (released as *'Til We Outnumber 'Em: The Songs Of Woody Guthrie*, 2000), Springsteen parodies himself, introducing his performance of 'Riding In My Car' by stating indignantly "automobiles... Mr Guthrie, no disrespect, but that's my business". Why give up an image that he has learnt to use so effectively? After all, the great Chuck Berry's entire career is based upon a mere handful of motorised anthems.

As for the stadium rock tag that has been hung on him since he toured the world with the ubiquitous *Born In The U.S.A.* during 1984–5 (and Springsteen undoubtedly enjoyed the success of this period if not the political misinterpretation of his work), it came on the back of the stunningly bleak acoustic demo-tape album, *Nebraska*, which told of serial killers and no-hopers. After the overblown (and arguably over-delayed, coming some thirteen years after his debut) live album release in 1986, Bruce then reigned back for the studio follow-up, the introspective and largely solo *Tunnel Of Love*, took five years off, and returned without his popular band in an attempt to explore new sounds. No simple following of the formula and cashing-in. Whilst he reconstituted the E

Street Band for more huge world tours from 1999, he did not rock out with a tour to promote his 1995 *Greatest Hits*, but waited for that year's devastatingly quiet *The Ghost Of Tom Joad* before setting out, travelling the world with just guitar and harmonica (actually, with a vast array of each), playing at theatres and even his old school. Every bar band dreams of selling millions of records and playing to as many people as possible, and Bruce has managed to achieve that. He has, however, always shown signs of humility and grounding by numerous appearances in the very bars he started out in, even stepping back and playing the guitar in a series of club gigs for his Pittsburgh soulmate, Joe Grushecky, in the mid-1990s. In addition, he has also continuously supported community charities and causes (in 2004 he held a book signing in New Jersey to aid local retailers!). Springsteen hasn't broken new ground in his career, except perhaps to carry over a liberal sensibility into the highest echelons of the mainstream, where many artists have either failed or instead become ghettoised. Steve Earle, a Springsteen fan and fine songwriter himself, sings aggressively of his own political feelings, and it is arguably this directness that has prevented Earle reaching beyond a strong core fanbase that shares many of his ideologies. He remains singing to the converted while Bruce reaches a far broader audience.

Frequently Bruce goes back, both physically and musically, to his roots and, whilst not a pioneer, he is an inspiring and powerful storyteller. He has taken the concerns of his heroes like Woody Guthrie and John Steinbeck, and even the youthful exuberance of Chuck Berry's car-bound characters, to a new level of success, familiarity and maturity.

1. Jersey Nights

Having spent his formative years as a musician in a host of wonderfully named bands – The Rogues, The Castiles, Earth, Child, Steel Mill, Dr Zoom And The Sonic Boom – based around the clubs of New Jersey and most specifically his adopted seaside home of Asbury Park, Bruce Springsteen finally landed his professional recording contract at Columbia Records, as a solo artist. The heavy metal and blues-rock fusion of Child – strongly influenced by acts such as the Eric Clapton-led Cream – had been re-branded under the moniker of Steel Mill. This group built up enough of a following to open for an act as well known as Grand Funk Railroad, whilst the subsequent Dr Zoom had landed a support slot for The Allman Brothers. However, with his new group, the horn-enhanced Bruce Springsteen Band, counting membership in the double figures, money was proving very tight for the young Bruce who was resolutely unemployed in a 'proper job', clinging to that of hopeful musician. Various band members had taken part-time work to make ends meet, while Bruce increasingly looked for solo gigs in the folk clubs of New York to keep himself occupied, and in money. Thus, it was when his original, informal manager, Carl 'Tinker' West, put Springsteen in touch with showbiz wannabes Mike Appel and Jim Cretecos, that he played solo and acoustic for them. This pair of occasional pop producers and song-writers, who had written a couple of Partridge Family hits, were undoubtedly dominated by Appel and, after a delay that forced Bruce to re-contact Appel to remind him who he was, Springsteen's career was taken firmly in hand. Appel had an unusually aggressive approach to promotion in which there was little space for subtlety and building relationships, and once he fell for Springsteen's act, he went all out to make him a success. He forced Columbia Records' legendary A&R man John Hammond to give his new client an audition through sheer cheek, insinuating that Hammond would be making a huge mistake if he passed up a chance to hear Bruce. The A&R man must have heard this kind of bravado hundreds of times before, yet Appel's manner was persuasive, even if it was curiosity on Hammond's part as to whether this upstart might just be peddling a future star. When Springsteen played his demo set on 3 May 1972 (widely bootlegged since and with some of the performances given an official release on *Tracks*), Hammond felt that Appel had indeed been right and this New Jersey singer was something special, particularly impressing him with a rendition of 'If I Was The Priest'. Just over a month later, on 9 June, Bruce Springsteen became a Columbia recording artist, signed by the man who had previously brought Bob Dylan's signature to the label. It has often been suggested that Springsteen was seen as a 'new' or replacement Dylan, whose own powers seemed in decline after a run of albums that had not been greeted critically with the previously mandatory 'classic' status, although *Blood On The Tracks* was just around the corner. Bruce, however, was a rock and roll fan at heart (as, ironically, was Dylan himself

16

despite being first claimed and then savaged by the folk purists). Bruce was devoted to Little Richard and Chuck Berry, the Stax and Motown label sounds, British invasion bands, and the great showman, Elvis Presley. Where Dylan's early lyrics – and indeed melodies – did draw heavily on folk music (1963's 'Girl From The North Country' strongly borrowed from the traditional 'Scarborough Fair', for example) and followed the civil rights political protests of Woody Guthrie and Pete Seeger, Springsteen sang of the everyday lives he witnessed being acted out around him. The nightlife and the curious street characters, his friends and all their dreams – this was a world in which he was an active participant and one that he found himself able to recount vividly in his music. Therefore, despite being keen to sign under his own name with a batch of songs he had specifically written to enable him to play solo gigs and travel lighter, it is no surprise to find various members from his recent past rock bands helping out on the debut Bruce Springsteen album, *Greetings From Asbury Park, N.J.*, rather than it simply being a vehicle for one man and his guitar.

From Asbury Park, N.J., 1973.

Produced By:
Mike Appel, Jim Cretecos.

Personnel:
Clarence Clemons, Vincent 'Loper' Lopez, David Sancious, Bruce Springsteen, Garry Tallent.

Additional Musicians:
Richard Davis, Harold Wheeler.

Songs:
'Blinded By The Light', 'Growin' Up', 'Mary Queen Of Arkansas', 'Does This Bus Stop At 82nd Street?', 'Lost In The Flood', 'The Angel', 'For You', 'Spirit In The Night', 'It's Hard To Be A Saint In The City'.

The urgent 'Blinded By The Light' opened Springsteen's debut, and first of two albums, in 1973. It was a torrent of surreal images and phrases that the twenty-three year old had seemingly thrown down for the primary purpose of connecting renditions of the lively chorus, although the writer's resourcefulness to find the endless rhymes is undeniably impressive. The rest of the album – and his previous two years of prolific songwriting and demo recording – reveal an artist learning as he went along how to tailor his cinematic storytelling and poetic imagery, streetwise and colourful characters to the medium of popular song. At their best the songs on *Greetings*, although flawed (far too many dense similes – "I've been a shine boy for your acid brat and a wharf rat of your state" he sings to 'Mary Queen Of Arkansas'), are undeniably passionate. 'For You' has even made a reappearance some thirty years down the line as a solo interlude in the E Street Band stadium shows, with Bruce at the piano, but, as part of the hook has it, "you did not need my urgency...". Tracks such as 'The Angel' and 'Mary Queen Of Arkansas' succeed in slowing down the frenetic pace, allowing the listener to catch some sort of breath, but even within the sparse acoustic strumming of these songs, the imagery is never less than gushing out, like oil from a cracked tank. Closing with the impressively swaggering 'It's Hard To Be A Saint In The City', Bruce may not have quite "burst just like a supernova" as the song has it, but this album is a very solid start from a man who had already written scores of songs but had yet to understand quite how to harness his writing to his chosen form of expression. Perhaps the record's biggest weakness is the undermining tension between Appel and Columbia's hopes for an acoustic collection, and Bruce's natural ease in the company of his musician friends and a band sound. Bruce has claimed that it was through Clive Davis' initial rejection of the album for its lack of obviously commercial singles that caused him to go and write 'Blinded By The Light' and 'Spirit In The Night', two of the more orchestrated tracks. Bruce may originally have been keen to be signed as a solo act but he gradually pulled in more of his past Jersey band colleagues over the course of recording, despite a reluctance for this augmentation by his manager/producers. Come the follow-up record, there was no doubt who had begun to win that battle.

Highlights:

'Growin' Up' – a warm, early anthem that has Bruce playing the rebel, but with great humour in place of brooding bravado that might have been expected from a young newcomer. Here he flies a pirate flag and takes care to look "just right" before, prophetically, he finds "the key to the universe in the engine of an old parked car"!

'For You' – densely packed with similes, as is too much of this album, this is one of the more satisfying tracks on the album for its passionate hook, despite an unclear narrative. The hospital imagery points to the object of the narrator's frustrated affection being in physical trouble, whilst there is mention of "your Chelsea suicide" to suggest an even darker aspect to the tale, as does the past tense of "your life was one long emergency".

Weak Spots:

'Does This Bus Stop At 82nd Street?' – here the lovingly drawn characters of the Jersey shore make way for a cascade of fairly minimal descriptions. There is plenty of early Bruce surreal rhyming and the song still sounds fun on those rare occasions when it makes a present-day concert appearance, but it also has the feel of something very slight, perhaps emphasised by being sandwiched by two epic five-minute-plus songs in the running order on side one.

Key Missing Tracks (official release status is noted in parenthesis):

'If I Was The Priest' (unreleased) – when Bruce wasn't singing of the colourful characters peopling the Jersey shore, he was transposing them to the Wild West or the Civil War, where they became soldiers or outlaws, still competing for women's affections, and which suited his filmic aptitude to songwriting. The still unreleased 'Cowboys Of The Sea', 'Evacuation Of The West' (a full band workout) and 'Visitation At Forth Horne' all use Western imagery. 'If I Was The Priest', however, combines this Catholic religious imagery, another popular early Bruce trait. The Virgin Mary runs the saloon and the Holy Ghost heads the burlesque show. Along with many of the scores of demos and outtakes from the early Bruce canon, this song is impressively structured, although probably not a track that would have added significantly to his reputation. As a song that Bruce felt confident enough to play at his Columbia audition, and the one that John Hammond subsequently commented had helped persuade him of Bruce's special talent, it is curious that this did not even make the final cut for the *Tracks* boxset and remains unreleased, whilst four of the first album's nine songs were included from this session.

As the bootlegs that Bruce went to court to suppress in 1998 revealed, there were a lot of well-recorded demos and studio run-throughs made prior to the 1973 album recordings. While many of these are more curiosities than classics, the dramatic content and cinematic feel to unreleased songs such as 'Lady And The Doctor', 'Southern Son' and 'Randolph Street (Master Of Electricity)' suggest that a darker and quite unique record could have been assembled at this time.

The Wild, The Innocent And The E Street Shuffle, 1973.

Produced By:
Mike Appel, Jim Cretecos.

Personnel:
Clarence Clemons, Danny Federici, Vini 'Mad Dog' Lopez, David L. Sancious, Bruce Springsteen, Garry W. Tallent.

Additional Musicians:
Richard Blackwell, Albany 'Al' Tellone.

Songs:
'The E Street Shuffle', '4th Of July, Asbury Park (Sandy)', 'Kitty's Back', 'Wild Billy's Circus Story', 'Incident On 57th Street', 'Rosalita (Come Out Tonight)', 'New York City Serenade'.

The follow-up to Bruce's debut album showed a growing ambition from the outset with its witty, sprawling and film-referencing title, *The Wild, The Innocent And The E Street Shuffle*. The artwork was also more sophisticated than the brash, small town feel to the debut's postcard-adorned front. Here, the cover featured a close-up of a reflective, distant-looking Springsteen, partially hidden in shadows and with his right hand fingers touching his lips and beard to obscure his features further. The singer looks thoughtful and the music within has a more assured feel, even as it heads into jazzy interludes. The shortest song on the collection is the opener, 'The E Street Shuffle', which still manages to sound quite epic whilst clocking in at just under four-and-a-half minutes, from its deceptively ramshackle multi-horn introduction to its funk workouts in the final quarter. Four of the seven songs last more than seven minutes with the closer running a shade under ten. The more relaxed feel to the Springsteen sophomore effort is largely due to the space injected into narratives that are very much mining the same ground as on *Greetings*, but which presented here seem to carry a real feeling of summer evenings, with the soft thudding of Vini Lopez's drumming, twin keyboards and a fuller role for

Clarence Clemons' saxophone rounding out the band sound. The sense of openness in the music is created by soul and jazz inflections, possibly due to a greater role for keyboardist David Sancious. He would soon jump off the E Street wagon on the cusp of its big break to form his own experimental electric jazz band, Tone, alongside another brief E Streeter, Ernest Carter. Here, however, he adds textures and bubbly solos that are quite removed from the more strident piano style of Roy Bittan, band mainstay from 1975, and Danny Federici's underpinning organ work.

Where perhaps *Greetings* suffered from a uniformity of tempo in each song – 'Blinded By The Light' was frenetic from the outset, 'The Angel' soporific – *The Wild, The Innocent And The E Street Shuffle* revels in changes of pace within the tracks. 'Kitty's Back' opens with a seductively wailing guitar part from Bruce, who handled all the album's guitars, backed by a gentle saxophone and drum parts for the first instrumental minute. The song is then taken into a low-key funky jazz mood before building to an exciting rhythm and blues crescendo over the next few minutes. Lyrically, this is nowhere near Bruce's strongest effort, but as a group piece, 'Kitty's Back' remains an exciting listen today, even while it is very much of its time and of a style Bruce has never gone back to.

The seductive keyboard and accordion (the latter courtesy of Federici who had missed out on *Greetings* after years serving in Bruce's early bands) on '4th Of July, Asbury Park (Sandy)', combined with a particularly soft and yearning vocal from the twenty-three-year-old Springsteen, bring this piece to life. Even as the narrative describes the characters' lifestyles as inexorably altering, with the world around them no longer offering the security and comfort it had once provided, there is a sense of huge affection for the town and its fireworks. However, "this boardwalk life for me is through", concludes Sandy's lover, and with the restless confidence revealed in 'Rosalita (Come Out Tonight)' – an energetic concert favourite down the years – Bruce, too, would soon be ready to break out of the Asbury Park boardwalks and Jersey streets to construct a record of more universal resonance.

Highlights:
'4th Of July, Asbury Park (Sandy)' – the delicate, warm romance of this track, amidst the images of a decaying town (Bruce's adopted beach home in New Jersey), is subtly orchestrated, complete with Bruce on recorder.

'Incident On 57th Street' – a less frenetic piece than much of the album, this piece has images of street gangs and their accoutrements, but with an air of times moving on for the protagonists. The closing call for Spanish Johnny to make "a little easy money" is taken to a more claustrophobic, intense level in *Born To Run*'s 'Meeting Across The River'.

'Rosalita (Come Out Tonight)' – one of Bruce's live classics. This energetic, mock-autobiographical lyric of a young musician pleading for the girl he loves to give him a chance against her parents' wishes (they are unhappy "cause I play in a rock and roll band") comes alive when seen in the context of the singer having actually become successful – the ultimate vindication and pay-off!

Weak Spots:
'Wild Billy's Circus Story' – this is a slight song, a little
reminiscent of the debut album's 'Does This Bus…' in the
way it interrupts the themes and, like the earlier song, does
so as track four in the running order, lessening the impact
of the whole. The playful horn beeping its way through
'Wild Billy's Circus Story' gives this the air of a children's
song (although the images are mournful and adult, with a
junkie and a lonely-faced clown making appearances),
incongruous to the tales of passion and streetlife that
permeate through the rest of the album. The final line of
"all aboard, Nebraska's our next stop" almost provides a
great link to Springsteen's 1982 album. But of course,
there would be three more albums before Bruce presented
the world with his sparse masterpiece, and his writing had
by then far outgrown this burlesque lyric.

Key Missing Tracks:
'You Mean So Much To Me' (appears on *Tracks*) and
'Thundercrack' (*Tracks*) – two epic, funky tracks that were
concert regulars at this time and that could have easily
taken the 'Kitty's Back' spot on the second album, and
perhaps injected more straight-ahead energy than the
skewed jazz of the song that made the final cut. The
former was eventually donated to Southside Johnny who
recorded it for his *I Don't Want To Go Home* album, with
Ronnie Spector guesting at the invitation of earlier
acquaintance, Jukes producer Steve Van Zandt.
'Thundercrack' was often the finale to Bruce shows in the
early 1970s, but was superseded by the tighter and more
satisfyingly rounded 'Rosalita (Come Out Tonight)' that
became something of an anthem, closing scores of shows

until Springsteen adopted classic rhythm and blues numbers to fill the spot.

'Seaside Bar Song' (*Tracks*) – one of Bruce's early car-themed lyrics, full of romance and optimism, and a nod to the influence of Bo Diddley, both musically and in a namecheck. Two years later, 'Thunder Road' sounds like a more mature, slightly world weary take on this, where again the narrator seeks to take to the road, but instead of enjoying a ride with a "pretty girl on a sweet summer night", the later narrator warns Mary that the "ride ain't free".

'Zero And Blind Terry' (*Tracks*) – here Bruce had dreamt up a *West Side Story* for New Jersey, taking his character observations into a less personal, fictionalised world, complete with an epilogue that suggests that the characters' ghosts can still be seen. Despite the fighting and implied sacrifice, this song is far removed from the gritty realism Springsteen had moved onto by 1978's *Darkness On The Edge Of Town*, but this gang fantasy has definite elements of *Born To Run*'s 'Jungleland'.

Born To Run, 1975.

Produced By:
Bruce Springsteen, John Landau, Mike Appel.

Personnel:
Roy Bittan, Ernest 'Boom' Carter (left band during recording), Clarence Clemons, Danny Federici, David L. Sancious (left band during recording), Bruce Springsteen,

Garry W. Tallent, Steve Van Zandt, Max M. Weinberg.

Additional Musicians:
Wayne Andre, Mike Appel, Michael Brecker, Randy Brecker, Charles Celello (strings arranged and conducted by), Richard Davis, Suki Lahav, Dave Sanborn.

Songs:
'Thunder Road', 'Tenth Avenue Freeze-Out', 'Night', 'Backstreets', 'Born To Run', 'She's The One', 'Meeting Across The River', 'Jungleland'.

With his career on the line, record company pressure, production and personnel frustrations, Bruce Springsteen miraculously emerged from seemingly inevitable rock oblivion with a wonderful masterpiece of an album. *Born To Run*'s success averted the prospect of Bruce returning to play forever in the Jersey bars he had grown up in. Whilst he is a man happy to acknowledge his roots, still making 'surprise' appearances to this day at local clubs and events, it is hard to imagine him knuckling down in steadier employment – a first real job! – at the carwash or factory, or in some such Bruce-esque line of work. Hidden behind *Born To Run*'s main apparent themes of friendship and trust (including the betrayal of these and the naïve belief in them, in the narratives of 'Backstreets' and 'Meeting Across The River', respectively), were the protracted efforts to actually record the album. 'Born To Run', the eventual title track, was committed to tape back in August 1974, but the final recordings for the album were not made until July 1975. In between times, the cut's drummer and organist had long since departed, to be replaced by the dependable Max Weinberg, and Roy Bittan who would later provide vital support and assistance to Bruce's re-emergence in the early 1990s.

Although it has been suggested that at one point Bruce considered the concept of sequencing the album to present the story of one day, including the sound of an alarm clock to open the record, every song on the released version has at least one mention of 'night(s)' or 'tonight', and this enhances a sense of mournfulness and the characters' blindness to the real situations present in many of the stories. The flawed characters of 'Thunder Road', where Mary "ain't no beauty" and the narrator "ain't no hero", open the record, contemplating escaping, taking on the world and winning, all the while acknowledging that there are no guarantees for them. They have seen too much time and opportunity pass them by to be certain of themselves or their chances, but they still need to try. The following 'Tenth Avenue Freeze-Out' suggests a positive alternative to the search for an escape in 'Thunder Road'. Whereas the earlier song had a character who had "got this guitar and… learned how to make it talk", here we find a musician revelling in his situation and the familiarity of his surroundings, celebrating the arrival of the "Big Man" – Clarence Clemon's nickname, for obvious reasons – in the band line-up and finding "the sidewalk's bright" – enough to enable him to forget the darkness outside. From there, however, the dark begins to seep into all of the stories. In 'Night', the after-work hours are what the characters dream of, offering the chance to fulfil themselves from the enforced drudgery of their daytime labouring. Ultimately, however, something leaves them "sad and free", even as they believe they are in control of their lives.

'Backstreets' is a complex and devastating remembrance of a relationship that ended so unexpectedly in betrayal.

Side two of the original record (before albums were sequenced with compact discs in mind) kicks off with the sublime driving power-pop of 'Born To Run'. Where 'Thunder Road' saw a man beckoning (first with a mournful burst of harmonica and an anxiously urgent piano, and then with a vulnerable vocal) to his prospective lover to take the chance and hit the road with him, 'Born To Run' hits the listener with its echoing layers of sound from the outset (an acknowledged pastiche of Phil Spector's Wall-of-Sound production technique), where the instruments all seem to be competing. Here, the characters are already out there in the "runaway American Dream", their "suicide machines". Again, they are looking to escape – "we gotta get out while we're young" – but, despite the triumphal singalong this has grown to be, with its undaunted statement of intent, "baby we were born to run", in truth, the characters find that the "highway's jammed with broken heroes" and the hope that they will someday reach their ideal place sounds more desperate than certain. Yet, it is hope that they can cling to that drives them on. As Bruce would later write for *The Ghost Of Tom Joad*, "what are we without hope in our hearts?"

The album continues with 'She's The One', borrowing a Bo Diddley-esque riff (indeed, on occasion, the songs 'Bo Diddley' and the similar rhythm-bearing 'Mona' have been used as introductions to this song in concert, seguing neatly into the Springsteen lyric). The song lifts the "French cream" and "French kisses" lines from the earlier 'Santa Ana', used to emphasise the eponymous woman's distance from her admirer. 'Meeting Across The River' is a curiosity and apparently a track that Mike Appel fought to keep on the final album. 'Jungleland' is a powerhouse finale to the collection, a towering epic of gangs and desperate night life, full of wonderful imagery from the "giant Exxon sign that brings this fair city light" to the uncertainty "between flesh and what's fantasy". From the opening moments of Roy Bittan's piano and the violin of brief band member Suki Lahav, wife of the album's engineer, and encompassing one of Clarence Clemons' most significant saxophone performances, the song is unashamedly melodramatic.

The album finally captured some of the intensity and drama of the Bruce Springsteen live experience and swiftly landed him on the covers of both *Time* and *Newsweek*. According to Bruce, the success went to his head one night to the extent that he jumped the fence at Graceland to try to visit his hero Elvis and tried to talk his way round unimpressed security guards by stating that his picture was on these national magazines. He never got to meet Presley and the song he wrote specifically for him – 'Fire' – would become a hit for the Pointer Sisters instead, as well as a concert favourite in his own repertoire.

Highlights:

'Thunder Road' – taking its title from the 1958 Robert Mitchum film of moonshining and the Mob, this is in fact a stirring song of the youthful optimism of ordinary people with big ideas. "You ain't no beauty, but hey you're all right" the protagonist tells the object of his desire.

'Backstreets' – an ambitious, epic story of friendship and

betrayal, with a satisfyingly full production that had been missing from his first two albums.

'Born To Run' – in his sleevenotes to 1995's *Greatest Hits*, Springsteen admitted that this song was a conscious attempt to write a great rock and roll song, and he undoubtedly succeeded. The melodramatic song pulses with energy and self-confidence, both of the narrating character and, clearly, of Bruce himself. Lyrically influenced by Chuck Berry with its car/road/girl imagery, vocally by the name-checked Roy Orbison and his histrionic delivery, and most prevalently by the Wall of Sound of legendary producer Phil Spector, the record would find its own place as a classic.

'Jungleland' – a film noir-influenced tale of epic proportions, telling of gangs clashing in the night with resulting destruction and despair amidst some wonderful late-night imagery. Clarence Clemons' saxophone solo remains a spine-tingling moment in concerts today.

Weak Spots:
'Meeting Across The River' – with a subdued jazzy trumpet and a decidedly downbeat arrangement, this piece does serve to set up the wonderful album climax, but feels undernourished lyrically.

Key Missing Tracks:
'The Fever' (*18 Tracks*) – for years this was known from the wonderful Southside Johnny recording – one of many Springsteen donations to his erstwhile New Jersey friend and rhythm and blues enthusiast, that he made his own

upon receiving. Mike Appel had circulated promotional pressings of Bruce singing this classic song of loss and desire and the final, belated, official release of this on *18 Tracks* was prompted by fans' disappointment at its curious omission from the *Tracks* boxset. With an album as familiar as *Born To Run*, it is hard to imagine an alternative track-listing, but this should have been an early hit single for Bruce.

2. Dark Currents

Following Jon Landau's addition to the production team
for *Born To Run*, Springsteen felt that his new friend was
the way forward in terms of giving guidance to his career.
He wanted out of what he had come to feel was an unfair
and unprofessional contract, signing him to Mike Appel
when he was young and naïve about the business side of
the music industry – and he wanted Appel out of his
future. Appel's Laurel Canyon Productions ensured a legal
bar on his recording with Landau whilst their legal dispute
with Springsteen was in process. Bruce sued for "fraud,
undue influence and breach of trust", amongst a host of
reasons, whilst Appel counter-sued mainly regarding the
perceived change of allegiance in Jon Landau's favour.
When the case was eventually settled (see Marc Eliot and
Mike Appel's exhaustive, if subjective, account in their
book *Down Thunder Road*), Springsteen and Appel were
formally professionally separated. The tussle had kept
Bruce and the band out of the studio for close to two
years, lost him invaluable momentum from the break-
through record, and saw an almost three-year gap between
album releases.

Darkness On The Edge Of Town, 1978.

Produced By:
Jon Landau, Bruce Springsteen. (Chuck Plotkin received a thank you "for his assistance in the completion of this album".)

Personnel:
Roy Bittan, Clarence Clemons, Danny Federici, Bruce Springsteen, Garry Tallent, Steve Van Zandt, Max Weinberg.

Songs:
'Badlands', 'Adam Raised A Cain', 'Something In The Night', 'Candy's Room', 'Racing In The Street', 'The Promised Land', 'Factory', 'Streets Of Fire', 'Prove It All Night', 'Darkness On The Edge Of Town'.

In 1978, Bruce Springsteen finally returned to the fray, from the prolonged legal battle with his now ex-manager, Mike Appel, and released *Darkness On The Edge Of Town*. While the album featured the wide-open spaces of its predecessor, the optimism of songs such as 'Thunder Road' and 'Born To Run' was far more elusive in this album's ten tracks. The legal fight seemed to have caused a sobering in Springsteen's outlook, and perhaps also gave him the time to delve more into the classic books and films of American culture that have subsequently informed his writing. There are certainly some stark references to the Old Testament and, where there is a strident belief of a "promised land", it is tempered by the need to head "straight into the storm" to try to locate it. Even the enjoyment of 'Racing In The Street' is merely a transient means of escaping the harsh reality of everyday life. Bruce revealingly notes, in his book *Songs*, that he "had a reaction to my own good fortune" and wanted a record talking about people who had little choice but to stay where they were and make the best of things. To be true to this uncommercial vision, many fine upbeat songs were left off the record, including 'Because The Night', a song that Patti Smith took to the charts long before a live E Street Band version would see the light of day on the *Live 1975–85* set.

Darkness did not mark a permanent bleakening in Springsteen's world view, but the writing of the album did see him adding an extra lyrical depth to his canon, focusing more on social concerns and realism. Throughout this period, Bruce's performances continued to be epic and ultimately life-affirming. For every new song like 'Factory', Bruce could call on an old favourite like the raucous 'Rosalita', or a light-hearted new composition such as 'Fire'. Rock and roll standards would also still be wheeled out as acknowledgement for the band's roots. The best way to be heard was to put on a show that truly entertained, whatever the subject matter. Despite being one of Springsteen's strongest collections of songs, its author has always claimed an unhappiness with the final production of *Darkness*. Perhaps as a reaction to the difficulties he had found in recording his last two efforts, Bruce's onstage right-hand man, 'Miami' Steve Van Zandt, was brought into the production team of Bruce and Jon Landau for the next project, the mammoth double album *The River*.

Highlights:
Nine intense songs that still sound fresh and powerful today, with perhaps 'Badlands', 'The Promised Land' and the title track the truly outstanding efforts, are all present and correct in the current live Springsteen experience. The latter two were superbly re-worked for the solo acoustic tour, emphasising the power of their lyrics and imagery.

Weak Spots:
'Candy's Room' – an exception to the broad themes of restlessness and resignation of everyday working-class life. The song is certainly full of desire, apparently for a prostitute, but also somewhat one-dimensional.

Key Missing Tracks:
'Frankie' (*Tracks*) – re-recorded for subsequent albums (the official release dates from 1982), indicating Bruce's fondness for this mournful yet romantic tale with a lilting melody. It was perhaps left off *Born In The U.S.A.* for some thematic, if not stylistic, similarities to 'My Hometown', including as it does the line "everybody's dying, this town's closing down". The slow pace of this track may have been too much for *Darkness*, which already had the centrepiece of 'Racing In The Street'.

The River, 1980.

Produced By:
Bruce Springsteen, Jon Landau, Steve Van Zandt. (As with *Darkness*, Chuck Plotkin gets a "special thanks", along with Neil Dorfsman.)

Personnel:
Roy Bittan, Clarence Clemons, Danny Federici, Bruce Springsteen, Garry Tallent, Steve Van Zandt, Max Weinberg.

Songs Disc One (as per CD release):
'The Ties That Bind', 'Sherry Darling', 'Jackson Cage', 'Two Hearts', 'Independence Day', 'Hungry Heart', 'Out In The Street', 'Crush On You', 'You Can Look (But You Better Not Touch)', 'I Wanna Marry You', 'The River'.

Songs Disc Two:
'Point Blank', 'Cadillac Ranch', 'I'm A Rocker', 'Fade Away', 'Stolen Car', 'Ramrod', 'The Price You Pay', 'Drive All Night', 'Wreck On The Highway'.

Famously prolific (in terms of recording if not releasing songs), Bruce Springsteen also had a stubborn method of recording primarily as live, certainly during the 1970s. Thus, a huge number of songs were laid down for *The River*, each with a startling number of takes. A bootleg circulated, purporting to represent the original 1979 concept of a single album (under the title *The Ties That Bind*) that came close to release. However, echoing the frustrations and uncertainties of the *Born To Run* sessions (and suggesting that Jon Landau did not hold all the answers – to which the disgruntled Mike Appel would attest), some of these tracks were ditched, and many more added, as the project grew into a double album. Miami Steve Van Zandt – having been the driving force behind the first Southside Johnny And The Asbury Jukes albums – was added to the production team to help bring the different strands of Springsteen's writing into a coherent whole. While *Darkness On The Edge Of Town* revealed a maturing of Bruce's lyric writing, it had confused some by eschewing the youthful exuberance of the first three albums, replacing it with a hardened cynicism – sometimes with a sense of defiance (as on 'Prove It All Night' and 'Racing In The Street') but it was always at the heart of the characters' lives. With *The River*, Bruce seemed intent on further exploring the darker themes he had found such affinity with, while also letting loose with some raucous, straightforward rock, reflecting the mix that left the audience gasping for breath after the typical three-hour E Street Band show.

The River contains some of Bruce's most impassioned character songs, with the title track a masterclass of insightful narrative within the rock song format, and a great vehicle for Bruce's smooth harmonica playing. Elsewhere, the record veers into ribald humour in 'Crush On You' and 'Ramrod', drifts darkly into the world of dreams gone bad in 'Stolen Car' and 'The Price You Pay' and has an unashamedly good time in 'Hungry Heart' (even if this details a man abandoning his wife and children!). Thus, *The River* covered all bases in Springsteen's musical world to date. The album could superficially be viewed as the perfect Bruce release, for the set includes some of his finest work in each style, but perhaps ultimately it overreaches and the mood shifts are too abrupt, giving an unfocused feel. Commercially, however, *The River* put Bruce right back to the top. The album was a number one hit and the twenty songs, with numerous unheard gems ready to be unleashed, meant Bruce's legendary live shows had strong new blood to pulse through them.

Highlights:

'Jackson Cage' and 'Point Blank' – in amongst the bois-
terous rock and roll of the fun 'Two Hearts', 'Out In The
Street' and 'Cadillac Ranch' are songs of people who have
been caught and worn down by their circumstances. Work
has taken everything from them, until they both depend
on and take it for granted.

'The River' – a true classic, fully highlighting Bruce's
adeptness at concise storytelling within a pop song structure. From a sublime harmonica introduction, the song
unfolds to reveal a stunning narrative of economics
souring a youthful romance (hard to imagine that Ronald
Reagan had heard this song when he tried to appropriate
Bruce's persona during the 1984 election).

Weak Spots:

There's a thin line on *The River* between simply having
fun and mindlessness, and on some days 'Ramrod', 'Crush
On You' and 'I'm A Rocker' are eminently skip-able (in
the CD age!). Still, they can be perfect for singing along to
at home when no one's around, or when you're hidden in
a massive stadium crowd with everyone doing the same!

Key Missing Tracks:

'Loose Ends' (*Tracks*) – a seemingly effortless melody, with
every part of the band contributing strongly, cushioning
the sad tale of a passionate romance inexplicably unravel-
ling. Thematically, it would have fitted with 'The River'
and 'Stolen Car' as a narrative of a relationship that has
slipped from the protagonist's control.

'Where The Bands Are' (*Tracks*) – a disposable and straight-forward song with the simplest of choruses (the title repeated over and over), but with the overwhelming love of rock and roll at its heart, it would have served better than some of the throw-away rockers that did make the long tracklisting.

'Take 'Em As They Come' (*Tracks*) – a disturbing vision of a man on the edge, who advises his girlfriend to bring along a switchblade for their meeting. The insistent chorus aside, this points the way to the *Nebraska* songs.

3. Fistful Of Dollars

With *The River*, Bruce had consolidated his position as a major commercial artist, partially threatened by the loss of career momentum after the heights of *Born To Run* caused by the legal dispute with Mike Appel. *Darkness On The Edge Of Town* was an unprecedented dark collection of songs, following the youthful optimism of the first Springsteen albums. *The River* became a somewhat bloated follow-up, seemingly unsure where to focus with erratic sequencing, but it was buoyed by the hit single 'Hungry Heart'. On Joey Ramone's death, Bruce commented that he had penned this track for The Ramones, but had been persuaded to keep this curiously upbeat tale of a father deserting his family for himself. On the next Bruce Springsteen album, unsatisfied and isolated characters would dominate, but there would be no rock and roll band to lift any tension in their stories.

Nebraska, 1982.

Produced By:
None credited.

Personnel:
Bruce Springsteen.

Songs:
'Nebraska', 'Atlantic City', 'Mansion On The Hill', 'Johnny 99', 'Highway Patrolman', 'State Trooper', 'Used Cars', 'Open All Night', 'My Father's House', 'Reason To Believe'.

Nebraska remains to this day a high-watermark in Bruce's career. It's an album that people who don't care for the mainstream rock image of Bruce can feel comfortable liking, highlighting as it does a masterful ability with narrative songwriting, stripped to the bone. The album is also probably the closest any contemporary performer has got to writing a modern update of the themes in the songs of Woody Guthrie. Dylan may have worshipped the man who wrote 'This Land Is Your Land', but very few of his own lyrics were as direct with their social conscience or commentary. The more recent Billy Bragg and Wilco collaborations on previously unrecorded Guthrie material, released as the *Mermaid Avenue* albums, were keen to highlight the perhaps overlooked variety of the man's songwriting, and paid considerable attention to the playful and lustful side of Woody. Springsteen's *Nebraska* is an authentic examination of working-class life, hope and despair. Peopled by the desperate, the lonely, the dissatisfied and the dangerous, this is challenging and satisfying material.

Beginning by writing and demoing a batch of songs at home onto a four-track recorder, Bruce set about working them into full band arrangements. The pure nature of the original demos enhanced the intimate character pieces, with their reflective viewpoints, and the songwriter felt this was lost in the hands of the full E Street Band, although ultimately these sessions have not surfaced for comparison. Disheartened, Bruce eventually had the idea that his home recordings were best suited to these particular songs and, despite record company reservations, the original tape was mastered and an acoustic masterpiece released. (The regard in which this collection of songs is held amongst fellow musicians was demonstrated by the unusual tribute release of 2000, *Badlands*, that featured cover versions of each of the *Nebraska* songs in order, with bonus covers of the original session outtakes. The collection assembled the likes of Chrissie Hynde, Ben Harper and Johnny Cash to record exclusive covers.)

Highlights:
'Highway Patrolman' – the anguish of a man's struggle to both do right by his wayward brother and perform his professional duty to society make this the most rounded and satisfying track on an outstanding collection of songs.

Perhaps because these were never intended for release and recorded in the ultimate of relaxed circumstances – in Bruce's own bedroom – the whole album sounds unselfconscious and the narratives of the lyrics are brought to the fore.

Weak Spots:
'Nebraska' – being hypercritical, the story of the Starkweather killing spree, having been filmed by Terrence Malick in 1973's *Badlands* (yet nothing to do with an earlier Bruce song!), is the least personal to Springsteen's memories and concerns of economic depravation leading to social breakdown and despair. It is, however, a fine exer-

cise in transferring and encapsulating a complex and harrowing tale into a six-verse song.

Key Missing Tracks:

'Born In The U.S.A.' (*Tracks*; re-recorded for *Born In The U.S.A.*) – whilst the concept of turning the batch of January 1982 demo recordings into a full-blown rock record was eventually abandoned, many cuts, including this from his post-*The River* songwriting period, would be revisited over the coming two years and emerge as the next E Street album. 'Born In The U.S.A.' was the most significant song from the home recording sessions that missed the final *Nebraska* album. Taking its name from a Paul Schrader script sent to Bruce with a view to his contributing a song, its genesis is a little confusing. Bruce had not read the script when he wrote his angry tale of a troubled youth's transformation into a Vietnam veteran who returns home to an unwelcoming society, he just used the title. Schrader eventually filmed the script as *Light Of Day*, after another Bruce song, and used Joan Jett's cover of this outtake instead of a new song. 'Born In The U.S.A.' in its original incarnation is a stark acoustic blues that allows no room for misinterpretation as a mindless patriotic anthem, as was the fate of the pounding, melodramatic version that was to become synonymous with Springsteen two years down the line.

'Shut Out The Light' (B-side; *Tracks*) – the officially released versions of this song were recorded in 1983, but 'Shut Out The Light' comes from the same general period as the *Nebraska* sessions, and one bootleg reveals a couple of the song's lines being worked on as part of the song

'Born In The U.S.A.'. Certainly it would have been a good fit with the dark reflective mood of the *Nebraska* album. Eventually released as a B-side to the 1984 full-band rocking version of 'Born In The U.S.A.', 'Shut Out The Light' follows the character of Johnny, returning from what we can presume is the Vietnam conflict. This time there is a caring welcome – from his partner and his family (who put up a banner, so conspicuously absent in its sister song where the character finds he has "nowhere to go"), and an optimistic promise of work. Ultimately, however, Johnny finds he cannot escape the turmoil in his own mind.

'James Francis Dear/Richfield Whistle' (unreleased) – a sad tale of temptation winning out in a man whose will has been weakened with the loss of his town's supply of work. There are shades of 'My Hometown' – "these jobs are going, boys, and they ain't coming back" – and the later 'Straight Time'.

'Losin' Kind' (unreleased) – Bruce's song titles have always shown a keen interest in film noir, but showing an awareness of this genre's literary debt, in his notes to Jon Landau sent with the *Nebraska* 'demos', he refers to this as "kind of like a James M. Cain story". Indeed, this downbeat tale of a man meeting a woman on Highway 17, picking her up despite his reservations and going on to commit murder during a robbery in an attempt to fund their new-found wandering lifestyle does have the air of inevitable retribution that exists in many 1940s noir fiction and movies. Propelled by a simple acoustic guitar strum with a tambourine keeping beat and Spanish guitar flourishes, this forlorn narrative would have added an extra musical dimension to the album.

'Child Bride' (unreleased; re-written as 'Working On The Highway' for *Born In The U.S.A.*) – a long, gently finger-picked song, fully realised in this version from the *Nebraska* 'sessions'. While its later reincarnation as 'Working On The Highway' would see it played for a somewhat manic and comic effect, this take is mournful and highlights the 'injustice' of the narrating character's treatment. He seeks the permission and goodwill of his girlfriend's father, but instead has to run away with her. Inevitably, they cannot escape the law (although in his words, "she was no younger than I been") in their romantic dream, and he is thrown into prison where he can reflect on his promises to his loved one and the best he can genuinely hope for. Minimal glockenspiel and harmonica are layered on the recording.

Whilst the acclaim for the album was good for Bruce the artist, it was not the hit follow-up to the accessible double album *The River* that his record label had hoped for. There were no chart-friendly singles to be found within this bleak film noir of an album. As with the enforced lay-off between his third and fourth albums, Bruce was in danger of losing the career momentum he had worked so hard for, this time through a brave artistic decision that he would release the album that made most sense to him rather than the logical and expected rock and roll record. Even Springsteen, however, was conscious that he would have to repay Columbia's faith by recording a more conventional album next time around. His task was to write a batch of songs that he could take to the E Street Band and have the confidence that they could do them the justice he felt they had failed to deliver for the *Nebraska* tracks.

Born In The U.S.A., 1984.

Produced By:
Bruce Springsteen, Jon Landau, Chuck Plotkin, Steve Van Zandt.

Personnel:
Roy Bittan, Clarence Clemons, Danny Federici, Bruce Springsteen, Garry Tallent, Steve Van Zandt, Max Weinberg.

Songs:
'Born In The U.S.A.', 'Cover Me', 'Darlington County', 'Working On The Highway', 'Downbound Train', 'I'm On Fire', 'No Surrender', 'Bobby Jean', 'I'm Goin' Down', 'Glory Days', 'Dancing In The Dark', 'My Hometown'.

Reports on the recording of *Born In The U.S.A.* suggest that Bruce had relaxed in the studio in terms of spontaneity, with far fewer takes for each song. However, post the aborted band sessions for *Nebraska*, Bruce Springsteen and the E Street Band spent two years, on and off, recording around a hundred songs before they emerged with the new full band album, consisting of twelve assured tracks. Opening with the militaristic keyboard motif of the title track, Max Weinberg's thunderous drums and a powerful vocal from Bruce, the album maintained this air of confidence and purpose throughout and had enough hooks to secure seven hit singles. The collection of songs was far from being one-paced and predictable, however. 'Cover Me', one of the least satisfying moments, had an unusual disco feel to it, 'Working On The Highway' was a rockabilly romp and 'I'm On Fire', a quiet and intense declaration of passion. Songs such as 'No Surrender' and 'Bobby Jean', curiously sequenced in succession, are in the classic Bruce theme of comradeship and loyalty, the former echoing strongly through the 1995 reunion with the reference to "blood brothers in the stormy night". A wry and affectionate take on growing up, the released 'Glory Days' excluded a verse that referred to the disappointment in the life of the narrator's "old man" who ruminates on "glory days gone bad". This segment would have linked the song more thematically to the album's 'My Hometown' − without it, 'Glory Days' is instead a great piece of slightly melancholic nostalgia, with a wonderfully fun singalong chorus. In between the two tracks is 'Dancing In The Dark', a number two hit single in the U.S., that has never been bettered in the charts by Bruce ('Streets Of Philadelphia' equalled this position in the U.K.). 'Dancing In The Dark' was a very late addition to the album, written at the behest of Springsteen's manager and co-producer, Jon Landau, who felt the album lacked an obvious single. The resulting lyric spoke of the hardships of a songwriter's life with its unsocial hours and writer's block, whilst the dominant synthesiser music tuned into the mid-1980s zeitgeist.

Unlike the timeless rock music of *Born To Run*, *Darkness On The Edge Of Town* and the country folk of *Nebraska*, the keyboard parts on *Born In The U.S.A.* give the album a slightly dated, less organic sound than previously and this has seen the album's critical approval decline in hindsight. The immense success of the record and huge subsequent world tour has made *Born In The U.S.A.* synonymous with the decade in which it arrived. The infamous cover image of Springsteen's white tee-shirted lower back, blue jeans, red baseball cap in right-back pocket and enigmatically positioned hands – all with a red and white background suggesting the Stars and Stripes flag – sparked much debate at the time. Accusations were made that Springsteen was being disrespectful of America, presenting his backside to the public, and, some suggested, deliberately inviting the thought that he was urinating on the flag. Others ironically interpreted the presence of the flag and the title of the collection as revealing a conservative patriotism. One of those who sought to utilise this viewpoint was Republican re-election candidate, President Ronald Reagan. In a rallying speech in September 1984, he summarised that "America's future rests in a thousand dreams inside our hearts. It rests in the message of hope so many young people admire: New Jersey's own Bruce Springsteen". Evidently, Reagan and his advisers felt safe in embracing a singer whose latest album, so stridently titled *Born In The U.S.A.*, had connected with millions of the youthful population. Unfortunately, Bruce's growing interest in politics during his career had seen him pen songs such as 'Factory' and 'The River' and the whole *Nebraska* album. In 1979, he joined Jackson Browne and friends in the *No Nukes* disarmament concerts and, in the early 1980s, having met Bob Muller of the Vietnam Veterans of America, he started to contribute to this organisation. On his latest album, he was singing of his disillusionment with a society that was losing its ability to unite, leaving the returning, confused fighter of the title track alone, and a community in disarray and decline on the closing 'My Hometown'. The accompanying tour then saw collections for local food banks made at many stops. Reagan had badly misjudged the man from New Jersey. Springsteen's obvious displeasure at the attempted Republican appropriation did not mean that he was yet prepared to overtly endorse the Democratic Party instead. Springsteen hoped his everyday actions and lyrics would indicate his world view.

Highlights:

'No Surrender' – a fast-paced song of loyalty and friendship, with a 1960s style, massed backing vocals and wistful lyrics. Beneath the defiant chorus is a darker side that finds "war outside still raging" and longs to return to a more comfortable and reliable past. (Tom Hanks quoted from this song in his Golden Globe acceptance speech for his role in *Philadelphia*, whilst 2004 Democratic presidential candidate John Kerry adopted it as a campaign theme song – this time with Bruce's approval!)

'Dancing In The Dark' – an atypical pop song for Bruce, apparently written at Jon Landau and Columbia's request for a sure-fire hit-single. It worked. Beneath the catchy veneer, however, is a current of frustration and desperation, and a close-to-home account of a writer's struggles. The song became a regular part of the E Street Band's set on the tour supporting *The Rising*, but was resurrected and given a rockier arrangement than in its studio guise.

'My Hometown' – a magnificently concise, if forlorn closer, where the narrator recalls negative events in his town's recent history and concludes that leaving a place where he has witnessed violence and economic decline is the best he can offer his young boy. However, he wants his son to understand that this is the place where his true roots are – it is "your hometown" he states even as he is considering exile.

Weak Spots:

'Cover Me' – sequenced to follow the powerful (and infamously misinterpreted) title and lead track, this sounds a little forced musically. 'Cover Me' has elements of 1980s disco and was one of several songs that Arthur Baker would have a shot at re-mixing for extended-version B-sides. They don't work and yet Baker would soon be lined up to produce fellow Columbia artist Bob Dylan's new album – *Empire Burlesque* – where he succeeded in badly damaging one of Dylan's stronger collections of songs in the decade, with clumsy percussion overdubs. Lyrically, this song is inconsequential.

'Working On The Highway' – a bizarre bastardisation of the *Nebraska* session's 'Child Bride'. Turned into an upbeat, hand-clap-filled rockabilly number, the lyrics – bar the chorus – are remarkably true to the original incarnation, yet here the narrator just sounds mischievous. In 'Child Bride' we are told "grey clouds stretch across the white moon" – on *Born In The U.S.A.* we get a comic proclamation of the girl's father that "she don't know nothing about this cruel, cruel world" and closing repetitions of "woo hoo hoo". Undoubtedly, it's a fun, rousing rocker, but, as with *The River*, the album's tone would have been better suited for consistency by the inclusion of any one of a number of outtakes in this song's place.

Key Missing Tracks:

'Seeds' (*Live 1975–85*), 'Sugarland' (unreleased) and 'This Hard Land' (*Tracks*, original version; *Greatest Hits*, 1995 re-recording) – these show that Bruce had been delving into the dustbowl world of Woody Guthrie's lyrical canon. He emerged with some fine contemporary takes on these issues of man's struggle to provide for his family by working the land, fighting against nature's unpredictability and financial restraints. 'Seeds' and 'Sugarland' are tales of particularly angry and desperate men, with the narrator of the former closing in on a violence that would fit him in amongst the characters of *Nebraska*, explained by his bleak description of his child as having a "graveyard cough". The farmer of 'Sugarland' depicts his wife and father as reduced to crying and staring blankly, while his farm's "sheds [are] piled high with the wheat we ain't sold". Thus, he contemplates setting fire to his worthless wheat fields. Perhaps the reverse of these songs' two lead characters, who cannot see anything but the cruelty of their predicaments, 'This Hard Land' opens with a similarly unhappy situation, with failing crops and a place so unfavoured that "even the rain… don't come 'round here no more" – but on the back of true friendship, it concludes with a burst of optimism. Even if his closest friend cannot ultimately meet up with our narrator, he is not damned but instead is wished all the best, with the promise of meeting again "in a dream of this hard land". The song has a life-affirming lyric and a beautifully restrained rootsy arrangement, with a memorable melody that follows a strong harmonica opening. The 1995 re-recording is the match of the *Born In The U.S.A.* outtake, but seems a somewhat redundant exercise, particularly when Bruce deemed the original of sufficient quality to include it on the *Tracks* boxset.

'Man At The Top' (*Tracks*) – a simple song observing a universal truth – that everyone wants to be their own boss – this would have suited the album arriving in the middle of Reaganism!

'Pink Cadillac' (B-side; *Tracks*) – a driving (!) rocker, originally from the *Nebraska* sessions, where its acoustic setting made its central theme of lust somewhat more sinister. The full-band electric arrangement and vocal take of the released version give it a playful eroticism.

'Wages Of Sin' (*Tracks*) – a slow-burning tale of a character who cannot understand what has caused his relationship to break down. The loss of the ability to communicate adds to his sense of helplessness and keeps bringing the narrator to mournfully see that he is condemned to pay the "wages of sin" of the title. This is a perfect companion piece to much of the content of the *Tunnel Of Love* album, where love has gone wrong and the protagonists cannot see a way out of the turmoil.

Live 1975–85, 1986.

Produced By:
Bruce Springsteen, Jon Landau, Chuck Plotkin.

Personnel:
Roy Bittan, Clarence Clemons, Danny Federici, Nils Lofgren, Patti Scialfa, Bruce Springsteen, Garry Tallent, Steve Van Zandt, Max Weinberg.

Additional Musicians:
Miami Horns (Richie La Bamba, Mark Pender, Stan Harrison, Eddie Manion), Flo and Eddie.

Songs Disc One:
'Thunder Road', 'Adam Raised A Cain', 'Spirit In The Night', '4th Of July, Asbury Park (Sandy)', 'Paradise By The "C"', 'Fire', 'Growin' Up', 'It's Hard To Be A Saint In The City', 'Backstreets', 'Rosalita (Come Out Tonight)', 'Raise Your Hand', 'Hungry Heart', 'Two Hearts'.

Songs Disc Two:
'Cadillac Ranch', 'You Can Look (But You Better Not Touch)', 'Independence Day', 'Badlands', 'Because The Night', 'Candy's Room', 'Darkness On The Edge Of Town', 'Racing In The Street', 'This Land Is Your Land', 'Nebraska', 'Johnny 99', 'Reason To Believe', 'Born In The U.S.A.', 'Seeds'.

Songs Disc Three:
'The River', 'War', 'Darlington County', 'Working On The Highway', 'The Promised Land', 'Cover Me', 'I'm On Fire', 'Bobby Jean', 'My Hometown', 'Born To Run', 'No Surrender', 'Tenth Avenue Freeze-Out', 'Jersey Girl'.

Mike Appel had wanted Bruce to follow *Born To Run* with a live album, to capitalise on the success that Springsteen had finally achieved and thus consolidate his position by playing to his great strength as a live performer. Springsteen disagreed. With his next commercial peak, Jon Landau and his label were able to persuade Springsteen of the merits of a live release. Rather than putting out a souvenir of the massively successful current tour, however, the decision was made to produce a boxset of live performances tracing Bruce and his band's career. The five-record (triple CD) collection opened with a solo performance of 'Thunder Road' with Bruce at the piano, taken from 1975, and worked its way through some intimate performances before heading into the massive arenas that were at Bruce's mercy during the *Born In The U.S.A.* tour. Starting in the mid-1970s, it excluded notable band members Vini Lopez and David Sancious who had contributed greatly to the Bruce Springsteen sound in his early days as a Columbia recording artist. Carrying through to September 1985 (including a number of songs from the final show of the tour) did, however, allow Nils Lofgren and Patti Scialfa to have their performances included on a Springsteen album for the first time. The album was swiftly ratified as having outsold all previous boxsets and shot to number one on the American charts (number four in the U.K.). Whilst there was still the feeling that albums of complete Bruce shows may have been more satisfying, the sequencing did attempt to convey the tempo changes – and sheer length – of the live Springsteen experience.

Highlights:
'Because The Night' – fans were delighted to have an official recording of Bruce performing the song he had

donated to Patti Smith in 1978 for her to complete (and record a rare hit with). An example, along with a number of Southside Johnny numbers, of Bruce gifting away a chart-friendly song.

'Nebraska', 'Johnny 99' and 'Reason To Believe' – these slightly broadened and band-enhanced arrangements of *Nebraska*'s stark songs, whilst far from rocking out, were interesting glimpses of how the planned E Street record could have sounded.

'Seeds' – a *Born In The U.S.A.* outtake that received a belated airing. Its inclusion on the 1984 album may have added a toughness that was arguably lacking amongst its fine collection of singles.

'War' – the attention (and blind bandwagon-jumping) given to 'Born In The U.S.A.' by politicians in the 1984 presidential elections may have been the spur that led the liberal-minded Springsteen into a more active approach to politics. The introduction to the thundering E Street Band rendition of Barrett Strong and Norman Whitfield's 'War' – even included on the hit single release – reveals an angry and disillusioned Bruce, urging his audience to be wary of their leaders.

Key Missing Tracks:
'Incident On 57th Street' – released as a B–side and on the Japanese E.P. *Live Collection Volume One* that also featured a live rendition of the debut album's 'For You', this version deserved a wider audience, showcasing the band's skills and, notably, stamina!

4. Walking Like A Man

The *Born In The U.S.A.* album and subsequent tour had left Bruce Springsteen as one of the very biggest popular music stars on the planet of the day, alongside Madonna and Michael Jackson. This was a height of stardom the Bruce of 1975, despite riding high on the covers of major national magazines, could not have imagined. However, the misappropriation of his song 'Born In The U.S.A.' had alarmed him. His marriage in October 1984, to the model and actress Julianne Phillips, required some attention away from the media circus that inevitably surrounded a colossal tour and Springsteen thus stepped back from the spotlight leaving the hugely successful boxset to do the talking for a while. When he re-emerged, it was in a surprisingly new direction, with a stripped back sound from the rock workout of his previous studio effort.

Tunnel Of Love, 1987.

Produced By:
Bruce Springsteen, Jon Landau, Chuck Plotkin.

Personnel:
Roy Bittan, Clarence Clemons, Danny Federici, Nils

Lofgren, Patti Scialfa, Bruce Springsteen, Garry Tallent, Max Weinberg.

Additional Musicians:
The Schiffer Family (credited for "roller coaster"!), James Wood.

Songs:
'Ain't Got You', 'Tougher Than The Rest', 'All That Heaven Will Allow', 'Spare Parts', 'Cautious Man', 'Walk Like A Man', 'Tunnel Of Love', 'Two Faces', 'Brilliant Disguise', 'One Step Up', 'When You're Alone', 'Valentine's Day'.

A 1984 Bruce B-side, 'Johnny Bye-Bye' detailed Elvis Presley's undignified demise and perhaps the King's sad story made Bruce more aware of his own mortality and wary of the consequences of stardom. The studio follow-up to *Born In The U.S.A.*, 1987's *Tunnel Of Love*, was a surprising and brave reinvention of sorts for Springsteen, turning away from being a global, anthem-playing super-star to a more subdued and introverted point of view. The album is coursed with a sense of restlessness, even in the superficially lighter and optimistic opening trio of songs. The acoustic romp of 'Ain't Got You', where the character is bemoaning a burning loneliness, is full of witty lines emphasising his wealth and there is a suspicion that he is rather too preoccupied with himself. This song, with its Bo Diddley-esque riff, is arguably sending up Bruce's own success but, as with much of the rest of the album, the writer's ability with his craft must be remembered before it is simply regarded as an autobiographical piece. After all, the collection that features 'Ain't Got You' is dedicated to his then wife, Julianne Phillips, although the relationship was to have ended within a year of the album's release.

Springsteen himself, in the insightful comments in his *Songs* book, draws a line between *The River*'s track 'Stolen Car' – where love swiftly and inexplicably turns to restlessness (and the suggestion of suicide in the extended *Tracks* version) – and the writing on *Tunnel Of Love*. The album was his first sustained attempt to address "men, women and love" as he summarised the themes in the *Greatest Hits* sleevenotes. This included examining the influence of formative parent–child dynamics on subsequent adult relationships in 'Walk Like A Man' and the mysteriousness of love that can provoke uncertainty – in much of the rest of the album.

The recording of *Tunnel Of Love* was, perhaps, befitting of the material, relatively low-key and intimate. After some reportedly scrapped sessions with country musicians in Los Angeles, Bruce made the record at home, as he had done with *Nebraska*, but here he laid down the songs in arrangements that included drum machine backing, which gives them an insistent rhythm and that could more simply be worked up into band versions. Bruce then utilised the E Street members, calling them in as required to flesh out the songs. Max Weinberg either replaced, or enhanced, the various machine parts, whilst Nils Lofgren made his first studio album appearance as a part of the band, playing a blistering solo on the title track and adding backing vocals, along with Patti Scialfa and Clarence Clemons, to 'When You're Alone'. This proved the only credited appearance for Clemons on the album and there was no place for any of his trademark saxophone solos here. Perhaps the writing was on the wall for the band. Even the long serving Garry Talent and Danny Federici, and trusted Roy Bittan, were largely sidelined, with the sleeve credits bearing the line "all music performed by Bruce Springsteen except where noted" – and there was very little such notation.

Highlights:

'Cautious Man' – the road no longer holds even the semblance of an answer for the character Bill Horton, who resigns himself with a "coldness… he couldn't name" to the fact that he will stay with his young wife despite his uncertainties over the relationship.

'Brilliant Disguise' – while it would be presumptuous to claim that any of the material on the album is directly autobiographical, the passion and bitterness of this song – on an album dedicated to his wife – suggests that there is certainly an element of the confessional in the lyrics of betrayal where both male and female characters are "lost in the darkness of our love". This is a rare *Tunnel Of Love* song that Bruce has paid attention to in concerts, post the Express and Amnesty tours. It was the only song from the album that made it on to the *Greatest Hits* set, and was again chosen, with the title track, for *Essential*, although the album as a whole is one of the most consistently satisfying pieces of Springsteen's career.

Weak Spots:

'Tunnel Of Love' – the metaphor of a theme park roller coaster ride for a relationship is perhaps a little lazy, although the crazy mirrors are a clever image.

Key Missing Tracks:
'The Wish' – this one *is* autobiographical! A deeply affectionate tribute to Bruce's mother and the support Mrs
Springsteen had given, enabling him to fulfil his ambition
– the wish of the title. This warm song has some lovely
images – of Bruce in "Beatle boots... [and mother] in
pink curlers and matador pants", and is a counterpart to
the masculine relationship themes of the album's 'Walk
Like A Man'.

Tunnel Of Love, although intentionally with its more introspective material not in the same rock vein as its studio
predecessor, still made it to the number one spot of both
the U.K. and U.S. charts on release. Four months later
(having given the induction speech for Bob Dylan's entry
to the Rock And Roll Hall Of Fame in January 1988), the
E Street Band hit the road for the Tunnel Of Love Express
Tour, this time with a horn section, in part borrowed from
the Asbury Jukes, in tow. The five-month tour would
almost immediately be resumed under the guise of the
Human Rights Now! Tour that Bruce signed up for in
May after persuasion from Peter Gabriel. The British
singer (whose band included ex-E Streeter David
Sancious on keyboards), along with Sting, Tracy Chapman
and Youssou N'Dour, shared the bill with Bruce who was
the de facto headliner closing a majority of the shows. The
subsequent few years, however, would see Springsteen
shun the limelight as he dealt with the breakdown of his
first marriage and the beginning of a new romantic relationship, with band member Patti Scialfa. In 1989, he
contacted the members of his band to inform them of his
decision to stand the group down in order for him to

explore fresh musical avenues. With this move, Bruce Springsteen further distanced himself from the glory days of 1984–85.

Aside from a number of guest appearances at low key club gigs in the period between the Amnesty tour and the release of his 1992 albums, Bruce Springsteen only broke cover to headline a major concert on one occasion. In November 1990, he played two charity shows for the Christic Institute, on the same bill as Bonnie Raitt and old friend Jackson Browne. Taking the stage solo and acoustic, Springsteen unveiled new arrangements of familiar band songs such as 'Darkness On The Edge Of Town' and 'Tougher Than The Rest' on guitar and occasionally, as with the latter, on piano. Bruce drew heavily on the *Nebraska* album, playing six of its ten tracks, perhaps anxious to have a group of songs ready-made for an acoustic setting, but he tempered this conservatism by treating the audience to a total of half a dozen 'new' songs over the two nights. 'When The Lights Go Out', a dark, paranoid description of a small town where betrayal is looming, and the light and affectionate 'The Wish', would not surface on an official release until *Tracks* in 1998, but three of the other debutants made it to the final cut of *Human Touch*. Ironically, the Christic Institute performance of 'Real World' in a stripped back, piano setting was a far more powerful and affecting rendition than its somewhat blustering studio counterpart, for all the latter's soul aspirations. Over production and a lack of subtlety would prove to be the fault running through much of the *Human Touch* album.

Human Touch, 1992.

Produced By:
Bruce Springsteen, Jon Landau, Chuck Plotkin, Roy Bittan.

Personnel:
Roy Bittan, Randy Jackson, Jeff Porcaro, Bruce Springsteen.

Additional Musicians:
Michael Fisher, Bobby Hatfield, Mark Isham, Bobby King, Douglas Lunn, Ian McLagan, Sam Moore, Tim Pierce, David Sancious, Patti Scialfa, Kurt Wortman.

Songs:
'Human Touch', 'Soul Driver', '57 Channels (And Nothin' On)', 'Cross My Heart', 'Gloria's Eyes', 'With Every Wish', 'Roll Of The Dice', 'Real World', 'All Or Nothin' At All', 'Man's Job', 'I Wish I Were Blind', 'The Long Goodbye', 'Real Man', 'Pony Boy'.

Critically reviewed as the more significant piece of work of the pair of albums Springsteen released simultaneously in March 1992, *Human Touch* was actually far more uneven and unsatisfying than its 'younger' sister. Whereas recording for *Lucky Town* had ostensibly taken the matter of a few weeks, the sessions for what became *Human Touch* stretched over a period of more than two years, with a number of styles and groups of musicians employed. Bruce had wanted to explore new sounds having freed himself from what he perceived to be the constraints and limitations of the E Street Band and its established sound. The loose idea for his comeback album (there was an eventual gap of four and a half years between *Tunnel Of Love* and the 1992 albums) was to create a 1960s soul ambience. To this end, Bobby Hatfield of the Righteous Brothers and Sam Moore of Sam and Dave were employed to add significant backing vocal parts. The muscular title track opened the album in confident fashion, but its six and a half minutes ultimately proved the strongest of the collection of fourteen songs. Others had their merits, but tended to suffer from a heavy handedness resulting either from some uninspired arrangements or being forced into an unconvincing direction. Lurching from the light-hearted satire of '57 Channels (And Nothin' On)' to the biblical and apocalyptic 'Soul Driver', both previewed at the 1990 Christic shows and, from the generic 'Man's Job' and 'Real Man' to the traditional children's folk song that closed the collection, 'Pony Boy', the album suffered from a damaging lack of focus.

Highlights:
'Human Touch' – this song announced Bruce's return with an assertive, keyboard-heavy piece depicting a man's longing for intimacy against the harshness of the world, in a similar vein to material on *Tunnel Of Love*. Released as a single taster of what was to follow, 'Human Touch' would in fact prove to be the highest artistic point in an over-reaching and unsatisfactory collection.

'Soul Driver' – featuring some good, dark Old Testament imagery to illustrate a character's desperation, this is the most successful attempt to capture a new sound on the album, even if it isn't exactly traditional soul. A lilting melody is propelled by two guitars and E Street alumni David Sancious on Hammond organ.

'With Every Wish' – this acoustic number provides welcome relief from the histrionic and generic sounding workouts on the album. It also indicates an unexpected move of the maturing and more reflective Springsteen towards drawing on natural imagery, rather than relying on the streets around him. Mark Isham's trumpet part greatly enhances the piece, whilst subtly echoing *Born To Run*'s 'Meeting Across The River' where the character has already rushed into a plan without pausing to "think first" and seems destined for trouble.

'I Wish I Were Blind' – this sounds like an old standard, perhaps because there are no Bruce hallmarks present and because the imagery ("cottonwood blossom" and blue-birds!) is so familiar. There is absolutely nothing original about this song, but the gentle melody and forlorn vocal manage to lift it into something very touching and believable.

Weak Spots:
'Cross My Heart' – actually a good bluesy lyric, partially adapted from a Sonny Boy Williamson song, and a good rhythm, but the two-chord guitar solo is risible and badly damages the track.

'All Or Nothin' At All' – from the partially borrowed title (from an old Small Faces number one hit), through to the extended vocal coda of the repeated title line, this has no charm, a vaguely bawdy wit, but nothing that marks this track out as deserving of a place on a Springsteen record over the scores of fine works that have bitten the dust as outtakes throughout his career. The same can be said for much of this disappointing album.

Key Missing Tracks:

'Over The Rise' (*Tracks*) – a subdued lyric (including a quote from film critic Pauline Kael) sung with an echo effect, emphasising the finality of the singer's loss, now with only his own company, over a simple bass-heavy accompaniment, this explores the same natural expanses that 'My Beautiful Reward' inhabits.

'Gave It A Name' (*Tracks*) – although the recording date of this is printed as August 1998 in the *Tracks* booklet, this enigmatic song's presence among eleven other *Human Touch* session outtakes suggests this to be a printing error. 'Gave It A Name' also features the same quote from Pete Dexter's fine novel *Paris Trout* that Bruce incorporated into the *Lucky Town* song 'The Big Muddy'. Here, the image of moral corruption being contagious is represented as a character trait of violence, seemingly inherited from a father by his son. An understated, simple riff plays out under a restrained Bruce vocal. Thematically, it has links to 'With Every Wish' but its inclusion on the final album would not have made sense unless it was accompanied by some of the other slower-tempo outtakes.

'Part Man, Part Monkey' (B-side; *Tracks*) – a witty telling of the 1925 John Scopes trial that highlighted the debate over the teaching of evolution versus creationism. The song features an invigorating and fun Bruce vocal and bounces along with a fine, spiky guitar part – and again featured the Springsteen/Sancious reunion.

Lucky Town, 1992.

Produced By:
Bruce Springsteen with Jon Landau and Chuck Plotkin. Additional production by Roy Bittan.

Personnel:
Gary Mallabar, Bruce Springsteen.

Additional Musicians:
Roy Bittan, Randy Jackson, Lisa Lowell, Ian McLagan, Patti Scialfa, Soozie Tyrell.

Songs:
'Better Days', 'Lucky Town', 'Local Hero', 'If I Should Fall Behind', 'Leap Of Faith', 'The Big Muddy', 'Living Proof', 'Book Of Dreams', 'Souls Of The Departed', 'My Beautiful Reward'.

Human Touch was compiled from the results of more than two years of intermittent sessions with a host of different musicians and the album suffered from an almost inevitable inconsistency in sound and feel. As the finishing touches were finally being made to the album – to Columbia's undoubted relief – Bruce fell under the spell of a track on the recently released Bob Dylan outtakes boxset, *The Bootleg Series Volumes 1–3*. Making a particular impression on Springsteen was the album's final song, a

1989 *Oh Mercy* omission, 'Series Of Dreams', distinctively produced by Daniel Lanois. Bruce has claimed that hearing this inspired him to sit down and write 'Living Proof', based on his emotions at entering into fatherhood. The resulting session to cut the new song was extended as, from there, a whole album's worth of songs swiftly emerged. The connection between the Bob and Bruce songs is not obvious, yet the freshness of the *Lucky Town* songs does suggest that a new freedom, after the painstaking and protracted few years of recording, was unlocked in Bruce.

Lucky Town featured, in 'Better Days' and 'Leap Of Faith', songs that gave thanks to the redemption of love. This theme is carried further in the commitment songs 'Book Of Dreams', a depiction of the eve of marriage, and 'If I Should Fall Behind', a simple lyric of trust (even to the extent that there will be complications ahead). This song has subsequently been opened up to include the E Street Band members in its declaration of loyalty, adopted for the 1999 reunion tour.

Whilst on release, the shorter record was given only secondary attention to the much worked-on *Human Touch* (that charted a place above its sister in both the U.S. and U.K.) – down the line most critics and fans regard it as a far more satisfying and rounded affair.

Highlights:

'Lucky Town' – here Bruce takes the theme of restlessness from the *Tunnel Of Love* album and plants it into an irresistible rock setting. The track has a very loose feel, with a fine drum intro from Gary Mallabar.

'Souls Of The Departed' – an anguished rocker who is lamenting the futility of violence. Sadly its relevance still resonates.

Weak Spots:

'Local Hero' – this self-aware country-rocker would have made a fun B-side and concert interlude, but its overly personal and legend-deflating nature fit a little uncomfortably on what is otherwise a mature and thoughtful collection of songs, largely addressing love and responsibility.

Key Missing Tracks:

After the wealth (in the sense of quantity if not necessarily quality) of material Bruce had laid down with various combinations of session players from 1989 to early 1992, Lucky Town was apparently a very rapid affair and no outtakes have as yet been confirmed.

With *Human Touch* and *Lucky Town* released, Bruce was keen to further explore his music away from the security of his old friends in the E Street Band. Assembling a backing group from some of the album's musicians and a number of session players, Bruce launched himself on his first tour since 1988. Despite the continued popularity of Springsteen as a live attraction, the rapid chart descent of the two new albums must have surprised and alarmed Columbia executives and Bruce's own camp. Therefore, when MTV approached the singer to record an *Unplugged* set for their popular series that had helped to restore the critical health of Eric Clapton the previous year, Springsteen agreed to what would be his first full television special. Unfortunately, for an artist who had been signed as a solo act, who had performed acclaimed acoustic benefit concerts in 1986 and 1990, and whose 1982 *Nebraska* album was regarded as a folk classic, at the last minute Bruce changed his mind at performing alone and brought along his current touring band for the show. A great opportunity to prove to casual critics that he was more than a stadium rock act was missed. Bucking the format of the show also robbed loyal fans of a chance to see a more intimate performance of their favourite songs.

In Concert: MTV ~~Un~~Plugged, 1993.

Produced By:
Bruce Springsteen, John Landau.

Personnel:
Zachary Alford, Roy Bittan, Shane Fontayne, Tommy Sims, Bruce Springsteen, Crystal Taliefero.

Additional Musicians:
Gia Ciambotti, Carol Dennis, Cleopatra Kennedy, Bobby King, Angel Rogers, Patti Scialfa.

Songs:
'Red Headed Woman', 'Better Days', 'Atlantic City', 'Darkness On The Edge Of Town', 'Man's Job', 'Human Touch', 'Lucky Town', 'I Wish I Were Blind', 'Thunder Road', 'Light Of Day', 'If I Should Fall Behind', 'Living Proof', 'My Beautiful Reward'.

Opening with the unreleased 'Red Headed Woman' – a fast-paced innuendo-laden acoustic number written for his new wife, Patti Scialfa – Bruce then called out "alright, let's rock it" as his band kicked in for a solid electric set dominated by the songs from the new brace of albums. A rocking 'Atlantic City' was a surprising choice from the back catalogue and was another glimpse at how a *Nebraska* song could be successfully handled by a band. Two other old classics, 'Darkness On The Edge Of Town' (one of Bruce's personal favourites) and 'Thunder Road', helped the audience swallow the large helping of recent material and were featured on the album.

Aside from the disappointment at missing out on the opportunity to hear Bruce reconstruct his classic catalogue as solo acoustic pieces (as he had proved he could do powerfully with arrangements of 'Born To Run' and others incorporated into the sets of earlier band tours), packaging-wise, the album was a mess. Two images of Bruce are featured on the cover, overlapping, with the larger – Bruce singing earnestly into a microphone whilst playing a black acoustic guitar – a little misleading considering the content. The back of the CD case, and the booklet, used an edit of the front's collage, with two shots of Bruce's head, the bottom of these backed by the arm from the other. Surely a third still from the television broadcast could have been used! Inside the booklet, a similarly shoddy piece of packaging saw the controversial (non-E Street) band listed twice, opposite each other. The release was planned as a 'Limited Edition', emphasising the fact that the album was merely a trailer for the 1993 European leg of the current tour, with all the dates listed on the back of the CD. Planned as a tour souvenir/advertisement rather than an important artistic statement as the *Live 1975–85* and later *Live In New York City* were clearly intended to be, it was therefore not surprising that the album's production ran to an edited version of the television broadcast on a single album. The official video cassette release of the concert included an additional five songs, whilst a laserdisc edition added 'Roll Of The Dice'.

Highlights:

'Red Headed Woman' – this previously unreleased paean to Mrs Bruce Springsteen is a fun and dirty acoustic warm-up, although it is sadly the only solo piece of the whole enterprise.

'Thunder Road' – a stately Springsteen and Bittan dominated arrangement that gives the 1975 classic a new identity, suggesting an added vulnerability to the characters' surface optimism.

'My Beautiful Reward' – slowed even further than on its mother album *Lucky Town*, the song's keyboards give it a haunting air. This version shows that it is a track that is strong enough to withstand changes to its arrangement, here turned into an elegiac finale – a curiously uncompromising choice to close out the album, contrasting with the more familiar Bruce showstoppers such as 'Rosalita' and 'Twist And Shout', and especially as the video release had the more obvious and affirmative 'If I should Fall Behind' as the final song.

Weak Spots:

'Light Of Day' – a long and messy arrangement that is used as a vehicle for Bruce to introduce the band. This is a style Springsteen has used down the years in his mammoth concerts, but on a record lasting just over an hour, repeated listening of this fairly turgid track is very wearying. (This is a shame, as the song had only previously been officially featured in the form of Joan Jett's cover in the 1987 Paul Schrader film of the same name, originally, and rather confusingly, to be called *Born In The U.S.A.* and for which the legendary Bruce track was first written.) Thus, one of the two 'new' tracks included on this curious release turned out to be a very unsatisfying experience, although the lyrics suggest a tight three-minute version may have yielded good results.

Key Missing Tracks:
'Roll Of The Dice', 'Local Hero', '57 Channels (And Nothin' On)', 'Glory Days', 'Growin' Up' and 'The Big Muddy' were all part of the T.V. broadcast, with the latter two winding up as B-sides to some CD versions of the 'Streets Of Philadelphia' single. It would be inaccurate to claim that any of these performances would have transformed the album into a classic of the live genre, but the warmth and energy with which Bruce and Roy Bittan tackle 'Growin' Up' as an acoustic duo would have given a welcome relief from the solid but unspectacular recreations of the *Human Touch* and *Lucky Town* tracks.

5. Shadows And Ghosts

When Columbia records suggested to Jon Landau and Bruce that they compile Springsteen's first ever retrospective, the idea of recording some bonus new material with the (once) trusted E Street Band arose. Within days, the idea had become a reality, the studio reunion captured in an official documentary by Ernie Fritz, *Blood Brothers*, later released as a video and DVD. Any true resentments from the band members to their long-time boss for so abruptly dismissing them six years previously were hidden from show as the musicians swiftly gelled, tackling a mixture of old lyrics ('This Hard Land' had first been recorded for *Born In The U.S.A.*), through to recent outtakes ('Secret Garden' was from an abandoned solo Bruce effort the previous year) and even the brand new 'Blood Brothers'. The latter was clearly an allegory for Bruce and his friends in the band, a tale of loyalty and trust even as the lyrics suggest uncertainty over the meaning of their current relationship, wondering whether "any of this matters anymore after all".

Greatest Hits, 1995.

Produced By (new tracks):
Bruce Springsteen, Jon Landau and Chuck Plotkin. (Steve

Van Zandt was an original producer on the re-mixed 'Murder Incorporated'.)

Personnel (for new recordings):
Roy Bittan, Clarence Clemons, Danny Federici, Nils Lofgren, Bruce Springsteen, Garry Tallent, Steve Van Zandt, Max Weinberg.

Additional Musician:
Frank Pagano.

Songs:
'Born To Run', 'Thunder Road', 'Badlands', 'The River', 'Hungry Heart', 'Atlantic City', 'Dancing In The Dark', 'Born In The U.S.A.', 'My Hometown', 'Glory Days', 'Brilliant Disguise', 'Human Touch', 'Better Days', 'Streets Of Philadelphia', 'Secret Garden', 'Murder Incorporated', 'Blood Brothers', 'This Hard Land'.

Greatest Hits contained eighteen tracks, featured an Eric Meola photo from the *Born To Run* sessions on the cover and completely ignored the first two albums as it aimed squarely at the floating or non-Bruce fan. *Born In The U.S.A.* dominated the tracklisting with four songs featuring from Bruce's commercial highpoint. The addition of bonus unreleased recordings at the album's end, following 'Streets Of Philadelphia' (making its first appearance on a Bruce album, although without the extended intro featured in the film and its soundtrack record), gave the collection a somewhat unwarranted late-period slant with basically a third of the running order coming from releases in the past three years or new tracks, if 'Murder

Incorporated' can be counted as such. Perhaps the intention was to prove that Bruce Springsteen had more to offer artistically, post-*Born In The U.S.A.*, and dispel any thoughts that this release was merely an epitaph for a once-huge star now consigned to the music business periphery. The patchy *Human Touch* and underrated sister album *Lucky Town* are each allowed their opening tracks to represent the post-E Street world of Bruce. As an artist for whom the overall theme of an album is more paramount than the idea of chart singles (well, he has never chalked up a number one, with 'Dancing In The Dark' and 'Streets Of Philadelphia' each falling one place short), a single-disc, double-vinyl, 'hits' compilation was never going to be fully satisfying. However, whilst it seems a shame to ignore Bruce's strongest expressions of his New Jersey roots, as exemplified by the 1973 albums, for the beginner a collection that opens with the unquestionable rock classic 'Born To Run' and features so many other great Bruce moments is certainly doing a fine job. Fans may have bemoaned the lack of early material, but they were at least able to hear the beloved E Street Band back in action alongside Bruce.

Highlights:
'This Hard Land' – a folky ballad in the Woody Guthrie/restless worker vein, but with a sensitive full band arrangement. Bruce contributes some particularly notable harmonica on the track.

Weak Spots:
The exclusion of anything from 1973's debut and follow-up albums, despite tracks such as 'Growin' Up' and 'Rosalita (Come Out Tonight)' being long-established favourites in

Springsteen live set-lists, loses a key chapter of Bruce's development as an artist. Just two songs from the radio-friendly selections of *The River* and no sign of the stunning title track to *Darkness On The Edge Of Town* are disappointments. *Tunnel Of Love* from 1987 gets a similarly raw deal, with 'Brilliant Disguise' alone flying the tattered flag of that forlorn masterpiece, where 'Spare Parts' and 'Tougher Than The Rest' – for example – as charting singles had strong cases for inclusion. The lead track of *Human Touch* was probably that album's strongest offering and thus merited inclusion, but its counterpart, the title track of *Lucky Town*, was a muscular workout that warranted more notice and was possibly more deserving than the selected 'Better Days'. The latter is a fine number, but hardly original in sentiment, especially considering Bruce had featured on a 1991 Southside Johnny album that took its title from Steve Van Zandt's own 'Better Days'.

Key Missing Tracks:

'Back In Your Arms Again' (*Tracks*) – this was another new song worked on by Bruce and the E Street Band at the reunion sessions and featured strongly, but not in its entirety, in the documentary film *Blood Brothers*. Its omission from the final album gave the track the mystique of a lost classic, although its eventual release on the *Tracks* outtakes boxset proved it not to be an earth-shattering addition to the Bruce canon, but merely a passionately sung tale of familiar lost love and longing. Still, there was unhappiness that further evidence of Bruce's current writing was edged out by two already bootlegged songs from the *Born In The U.S.A.* sessions being re-recorded/remixed twelve years on.

Recording for *Greatest Hits* did not prove an immediate return to business as usual for Bruce and his old outfit. Bruce soon went off to work as a producer for Joe Grushecky and his band *American Babylon*, and then to record another intimate, largely acoustic 'solo' album, with minimal instrumentation, for the rest of the year.

The Ghost Of Tom Joad, 1995.

Produced By:
Bruce Springsteen, Chuck Plotkin.

Personnel:
Jennifer Condos, Danny Federici, Jim Hanson, Lisa Lowell, Gary Mallabar, Chuck Plotkin, Marty Rifkin, Bruce Springsteen, Gary Tallent, Soozie Tyrell.

Songs:
'The Ghost Of Tom Joad', 'Straight Time', 'Highway 29', 'Youngstown', 'Sinaloa Cowboys', 'The Line', 'Balboa Park', 'Dry Lightning', 'The New Timer', 'Across The Border', 'Galveston Bay', 'My Best Was Never Good Enough'.

Confounding fan expectations has been a common by-product of Bruce Springsteen following his artistic muse throughout his career. The rock and roll bravado of *Born To Run* made way for the disillusioned characters of *Darkness On The Edge Of Town*. Bruce had taken the unprecedented step of not only adopting the darker elements of *The River*'s lyrics for his next piece of work, but of keeping them unadorned in their demo form for release as *Nebraska*. The bleakly introspective *Tunnel Of Love* succeeded Springsteen's 'Glory Days' of 1984. Thus, the tantalising reunion with the E Street Band should not have been seen as an indication of his next move.

Unlike *Nebraska*, which had eventually emerged as a solo album after Bruce's despair at unsatisfying band sessions, Bruce intentionally recorded *The Ghost Of Tom Joad* acoustically, recruiting a small group of musicians to add extra textures to the songs. From the striking impressionistic artwork of the cover, with suggestions of blood and mud over a tanned human's back, to the minimal melodies on many of the tracks, Bruce succeeded in taking his personality out of these songs and bringing his characters to the fore. The lives Bruce is describing are on the edge, sometimes literally, with the Mexican border looming large in these tales of immigrants and lost souls. The title track, opening the album in a burst of harmonica, borrows Tom Joad's promise of hope from John Steinbeck's *The Grapes Of Wrath* (Bruce actually credits John Ford's movie adaptation on the sleeve), but Springsteen's descriptions of the homeless and lost are summarised by the bitter note of 'welcome to the new world order'. Most of the stories collected here are describing people in dead-end situations, alone and abandoned. As the chorus of 'The Ghost Of Tom Joad' has it, "the highway is alive tonight, but nobody's kiddin' nobody about where it goes" – the album's characters are all searching for something; a better life, lost lovers, or a sense of purpose, but they have to make the hard decisions for themselves. Tom Joad's principles are an example to them, but they are ultimately on their own and do not have the strength to pull themselves out of their circumstances.

The album is remarkably quiet and Bruce's vocals are unusually understated and low in the mix. With these elements, 'Youngstown' stands out for its fuller band sound. Soozie Tyrell's violin is particularly effective in mournfully driving the narrative of a town's fading and neglected history along, whilst 'Across The Border', again one of the more accessible moments for its fuller sound and unusually optimistic lyrics, suggests that some are able to escape their predicaments successfully. The writing on the album has a journalistic feel and often *The Ghost Of Tom Joad* sounds more like an aural documentary or short story collection than a record – this is a significant difference in style to *Nebraska* against which reviewers were quick to compare it. This effect can be explained by Bruce's inclusion of a list of sources from which he drew inspiration, featuring newspaper articles and books. This was some way from 'Ramrod' and 'Man's Job', proving how diverse an artist Bruce could be.

Highlights:

'The Ghost Of Tom Joad' – with a strident harmonica part from Bruce, the suggestion seems to be that now, more than ever, a fair and fighting character like Joad is needed, but there seems little chance for him.

'Youngstown' – this tale of the mining community of Youngstown and its contributions to America is one of the most impressive tracks on the album. Encapsulating nearly two hundred years of history into a narrative of economic downturn, Bruce does not glamorise the mining life that is being destroyed. It is painted as something "that'd suit the devil as well", but the song shows its past importance and the sense of purpose that is being taken away by its decline.

'Galveston Bay' – with a particularly minimal guitar accompaniment, this is a tale of prejudice and revenge, tempered by a final moment of understanding humanity.

Weak Spots:
'My Best Was Never Good Enough' – as with *Human Touch*, Bruce included a lighter song (although in this case there is a definite edge of bitterness) to close the album. After stark Raymond Carver-esque story-songs of migrant workers and ex-cons trying to make sense of their lives and get from day to day, this effort makes for a slightly unsatisfactory ending. The song is quietly amusing (and some suggested its listing of clichés was a response to the patronising patriotism implied within the Oscar-strewn film *Forrest Gump* of the previous year) but ultimately it detracts from the documentary feel of the album.

Key Missing Tracks:
No outtakes from the Ghost sessions are known as yet. The subsequent acoustic tour did, however, include some powerful new songs written around the same time as the album or during the tour itself. The strongest of these were 'The Hitter', a sad tale of a corrupt fighter adrift from the world, loved ones and even his own self-respect, and 'Long Time Coming', detailing the acceptance of responsibility of a parent who is determined that his children should make their own mistakes. Both deserve to be heard by a wider audience than the lucky few who were treated to their rare outings in 1996.

Making an acoustic album, in *The Ghost Of Tom Joad*, Bruce felt confident enough to embark on his long-cherished idea of a solo acoustic world tour. The intimate small venues and theatres that hosted these Bruce concerts witnessed memorable nights. Bruce interwove his new material with dramatically re-arranged back-catalogue classics seamlessly. Overcoming the worry that fans would not accept this unplugged model, Bruce injected moments of humour into the events and, deflating his genuine concern about distracting noises during his quiet set, he would threaten to come down and slap anyone who left their mobile phones switched on. A number of risqué – and not very good – songs were also thrown into the mix to ensure the proceedings were not too overwhelming. The tour was a triumph, but sadly, no comprehensive release has been made to commemorate it, with just a handful of live B-sides emerging. As always, bootlegs – of an extremely high quality – abounded, snapped up by eager fans (who would nonetheless have gladly paid again for an official album), but these live sets should have been heard by so many more, as proof of Springsteen's raw songwriting ability beneath what some perceive as his musical bombast.

Having ceased work on a follow-up album, believing that the work he had completed was covering no new ground, Bruce re-submerged himself into family life with his young children. The compiling of the *Greatest Hits* set, however, had seen him take a concentrated look back on his career and the inclusion there of two old, unreleased songs meant that he had delved deeper than the famous albums. The *Tracks* outtakes project of 1998 was the culmination of this ruminating on the past.

Tracks, 1998.

Project Produced By:
Bruce Springsteen, Chuck Plotkin.

Personnel:
Various.

Songs Disc One (all previously unreleased unless noted):
'Mary Queen Of Arkansas'★, 'It's Hard To Be A Saint In The City'★, 'Growin' Up'★, 'Does This Bus Stop At 82nd Street?'★, 'Bishop Danced', 'Santa Ana', 'Seaside Bar Song', 'Zero And Blind Terry', 'Linda Let Me Be The One', 'Thundercrack', 'Rendezvous', 'Give The Girl A Kiss', 'Iceman', 'Bring On The Night', 'So Young And In Love', 'Hearts Of Stone'.

Songs Disc Two:
'Restless Nights', 'A Good Man Is Hard To Find (Pittsburgh)', 'Roulette'#, 'Dollhouse', 'Where The Bands Are', 'Loose Ends', 'Living On The Edge Of The World', 'Wages Of Sin', 'Take 'Em As They Come', 'Be True'#, 'Ricky Wants A Man Of Her Own', 'I Wanna Be With You', 'Mary Lou', 'Stolen Car'★, 'Born In The U.S.A.'★, 'Johnny Bye Bye'#, 'Shut Out The Light'#.

Songs Disc Three:
'Cynthia', 'My Love Will Not Let You Down', 'This Hard Land'★, 'Frankie', 'TV Movie', 'Stand On It'#, 'Lion's Den', 'Car Wash', 'Rockaway The Days', 'Brothers Under The Bridges ('83)', 'Man At The Top', 'Pink Cadillac'#, 'Two For The Road'#, 'Janey Don't You Lose Heart'#,

'When You Need Me', 'The Wish', 'The Honeymooners', 'Lucky Man'#.

Songs Disc Four:
'Leavin' Train', 'Seven Angels', 'Gave It A Name', 'Sad Eyes', 'My Lover Man', 'Over The Rise', 'When The Lights Go Out', 'Loose Change', 'Trouble In Paradise', 'Happy', 'Part Man, Part Monkey'#, 'Goin' Cali', 'Back In Your Arms', 'Brothers Under The Bridge'.
* = alternate version of released song.
# = previously released B-side.

Tracks was originally announced as a project due to run to over one hundred songs and across six CDs, and promising to be something akin to the Holy Grail for long-term Bruce Springsteen fans. Jon Landau had persuaded Bruce of the benefits of going back to the original master tapes of each song they selected and remixing with modern technology to ensure the best sound – three teams of engineers were employed (one for each 'era' of recording). Occasionally, an overdub was required and even Vini Lopez was called in to play over tracks he had first recorded twenty-five years previously. Sadly, record company deadlines, with Christmas sales in mind, saw the set eventually cut by a third. This news put a dampener on fan expectations, anxious as to what gems had been returned to the vaults.

When *Tracks* was finally unleashed, it was ironic that, for such a long-awaited and highly anticipated release, the set opened in extremely disappointing fashion with four audition takes of songs that featured in very similar form on *Greetings From Asbury Park, N.J.* Springsteen explained away the absence of some bootleg favourites by saying the boxset was kept to a strict policy of only including songs recorded for album projects, yet these openers were most definitely never intended for release. Elsewhere, the inclusion of live takes of 'Bishop Danced' and 'Rendezvous' (however superior they may have been to any studio takes that existed), the inconsistent cherry-picking of B-sides, the decision to include two versions of the same minor song in 'Be True' and 'Mary Lou' and, most irritatingly, the inconsistency in chronology were all disappointments. Presumably, the latter can be explained by a desire to make the four CD set flow better as a listening experience, but someone who has forked out for this weighty boxset would be eagerly awaiting each hidden treasure from Springsteen, rather than treating *Tracks* as a thematic album itself.

Highlights:
(Listed previously with albums from which they were originally omitted.)

Weak Spots (with album they were omitted from noted):
'So Young And In Love' (*Born To Run*), 'Give The Girl A Kiss' (*Darkness On The Edge Of Town*), 'Be True', 'Mary Lou' and 'Bring On The Night', (all *The River*) – simplistic and lightweight 'boy and girl' songs that have moments of fun, but are unmemorable. 'Bring On The Night' reveals part of Bruce's songwriting process as he would retain and recycle a couple of its lines, incorporating them into 'My Love Will Not Let You Down' recorded three years later.

'Leavin' Train' and 'Seven Angels' (both *Human Touch*) – these mundane, plodding rockers were a poor start to a final disc that actually includes many intriguing efforts to expand Bruce's songwriting range and sound, such as 'My Lover Man', 'Goin' Cali' and 'Trouble In Paradise'.

Key Missing Tracks:
'The Big Payback', '30 Days Out' and 'Missing' were all omitted despite the presence of all the other studio B-sides. There were no studio versions of original songs only available in live form, such as 'Because The Night', 'Fire' and 'Light Of Day'.

Cornerstones of Bruce bootlegs, 'The Fever' and 'The Promise', were the highest profile absentees. Time constraints may have halted attempts to overcome technical difficulties with Bruce claiming to be unhappy about their sound quality.

18 Tracks, 1999.

Project Produced By:
Bruce Springsteen, Chuck Plotkin.

Personnel:
Various.

Songs (taken from Tracks):
'Growin' Up', 'Seaside Bar Song', 'Rendezvous', 'Hearts Of Stone', 'Where The Bands Are', 'Loose Ends', 'I Wanna Be With You', 'Born In The U.S.A.', 'My Love Will Not Let You Down', 'Lion's Den', 'Pink Cadillac', 'Janey Don't You Lose Heart', 'Sad Eyes', 'Part Man, Part Monkey', 'Trouble River'*, 'Brothers Under The Bridge', 'The

Fever'*, 'The Promise'*.
* = exclusive to compilation.

Released five months after its parent album, *18 Tracks* was a reasonable summation of the boxset, offering the more casual fan the chance to hear the acoustic blues version of 'Born In The U.S.A.' and the soulful 'Hearts Of Stone' at a more accessible price. The inclusion of three 'bonus tracks' was, however, a curious decision, solely appealing to the ardent fans who would have already bought the box. The presence of 'The Fever' made its omission from *Tracks* all the harder to understand, while 'The Promise' was a brand new version.

Highlights:
'The Fever' and 'The Promise' – these two legendary songs finally gained an official release, although the latter was re-recorded specifically for this sampler and its solo piano arrangement was played on the 1999–2000 tour. Bootlegs of the 1977 band version of this song of betrayal (held as an allegorical comment on the legal turmoil between Springsteen and Mike Appel) sound perfectly acceptable and aptly disillusioned with its cracked Bruce vocal.

Weak Spots:
'Trouble River' – this bonus track passes the time with tongue-in-cheek imagery, but it was certainly not the Holy Grail of a track that could have miraculously breathed the requisite life into the lacklustre *Human Touch*. Not in the same class as a majority of the songs not selected to represent the boxset and inferior to Bob

Dylan's own Bruce parody for the Traveling Wilburys, 'Tweeter And The Monkey Man'.

Key Missing Tracks:
In distilling highlights of a box of sixty-six songs onto a single CD, many very worthy potential inclusions were inevitably overlooked, with time considerations overriding artistic merit.

6. Rising Star

Bruce Springsteen had started the 1990s estranged from his brotherhood of the E Street Band, concentrating on his new wife, Patti Scialfa, and their growing family (they had three children in the early part of the decade), and recording with little focus, as evidenced by the resulting brace of albums released in 1992. Entering the twenty-first century, things were looking decidedly better for Bruce fans. Springsteen and Patti were very happily married but, additionally, Bruce had reactivated his old band and taken to the road in support of the back-catalogue trawling that was the *Tracks* project. The world tour, with both Miami Steve and Nils Lofgren in tow to emphasise the comradeship and support that the band had always stood for in the eyes of its audience, was heralded as a triumph. The setlists mixed the classics with the 'secret history' that the outtakes box had finally unveiled. The tour eventually culminated in a record-breaking ten stand in New York's Madison Square Gardens.

Live In New York City, 2001.

Produced By:
Bruce Springsteen, Chuck Plotkin.

Personnel:
Roy Bittan, Clarence Clemons, Danny Federici, Nils Lofgren, Patti Scialfa, Bruce Springsteen, Garry Tallent, Steve Van Zandt, Max Weinberg.

Songs Disc One:
'My Love Will Not Let You Down', 'Prove It All Night', 'Two Hearts', 'Atlantic City', 'Mansion On The Hill', 'The River', 'Youngstown', 'Murder Incorporated', 'Badlands', 'Out In The Street', 'Born To Run'.

Songs Disc Two:
'Tenth Avenue Freeze-Out', 'Land Of Hope And Dreams', 'American Skin (41 Shots)', 'Lost In The Flood', 'Born In The U.S.A.', 'Don't Look Back', 'Jungleland', 'Ramrod', 'If I Should Fall Behind'.

Bruce Springsteen's reputation was built on the back of powerful and legendarily generous live shows, with two-hour concerts considered 'short'. It was, therefore, a constant source of disappointment and frustration to fans that the only documents of the live Bruce experience were a fine but disjointed boxset and an unsatisfactory studio-bound MTV television show tie-in. The release of *Live In New York City* sought to address this by combining the best performances from two of the closing nights at Madison Square Gardens, to assemble a representation of the 1999–2000 Bruce Springsteen and the E Street Band concert. Utilising an image of Bruce and Clarence striking typical poses in black silhouette and a fussy colour scheme and graphic, the album's sleeve could have been for a show twenty years before. The recording and tour dates were not included in the title, an indication that the management were not going to relent and start issuing official 'bootleg' albums for each show or even each tour – this would stand as the full concert Bruce album for some time to come.

Highlights:
'Mansion On The Hill' – Bruce gave this *Nebraska* track a quietly dignified and countrified setting, featuring Danny Federici on accordion and Nils Lofgren on pedal steel guitar. Patti's distinctive vocal is allowed more space than often and effectively combines as a duet with Bruce to add a slightly mournful, poignantly nostalgic tone.

'Youngstown' – the most fully orchestrated song on *The Ghost Of Tom Joad* is taken over by the E Street Band who play a blistering arrangement, complete with a standout Nils Lofgren solo.

'Land Of Hope And Dreams' – lyrically, this new song borrows heavily from Curtis Mayfield's 'People Get Ready' and from traditional folk and gospel songs, with its imagery of trains and theme of redemption for all. There is also an obvious echo of Woody Guthrie's 'This Land Is Your Land', a song that Bruce had previously covered in concert and included on *Live 1975–85*. Despite simplistic lyrics, the song's irresistible rhythm carried it on for over eight minutes, as a crowd-pleasing and emotional showstopper.

'American Skin (41 Shots)' – an unusually direct 'issue' song from Bruce, this quickly became a key song in his latter-day output. An account of the New York police killing of an unarmed suspect, Amadou Diallo, fired on with the incredible number of shots given in the title, the song builds from the simple line of "forty-one shots" delivered solo by each of four band members before Bruce steps up to the microphone to draw them together. The song depicts the events that led up to the shooting, facts that were a matter of public record. Despite this, Bruce was accused of – well, some pretty bizarre and offensive accusations and insults were hurled at him from official police representatives who called for the boycotting of his shows and asked for officers who regularly moonlighted as concert security guards to stay away. The song was, ironically, a reminder that American society still had much work to do to be rid of its unpleasant residue of racism and intolerance.

'Lost In The Flood' – this darkly enigmatic epic from the debut album was a surprise inclusion during the tour and its muscular treatment breathed new life into its violent imagery.

Weak Spots:
Muddled packaging that took as its base the original television broadcast and thus listed thirteen songs, with six "additional performances", which make the album look like an afterthought. Peculiarly, there is no mention of 'Born To Run', a late addition to the set (and excluded from white label preview copies) that closes disc one of the double-CD set and which might have induced some more cautious fans to give a live Springsteen album a chance.

While the reunion tour had proved a huge commercial hit and the band's playing had impressed Bruce, a studio release was not going to be rushed out, with occasional recording sessions allowing the band a chance to interact in the studio. Then the horrors of September 11th 2001 took control of world events. The tragic events of that day, and the varying personal, media and government reactions, focused Bruce Springsteen's writing and within a year he had emerged with the thoughtful and powerful album *The Rising*, featuring the full E Street Band for the first time since *Born In The U.S.A.* in 1984.

The Rising, 2002.

Produced By:
Brendan O'Brien.

Personnel:
Roy Bittan, Clarence Clemons, Danny Federici, Nils Lofgren, Patti Scialfa, Bruce Springsteen, Garry Tallent, Steve Van Zandt, Max Weinberg.

Additional Musicians:
Asif Ali Khan and Group, Alliance Singers, Jere Flint, Larry Lemaster, Nashville String Machine, Brendan O'Brien, Jane Scarpantoni, Soozie Tyrell. Additional horns on 'Mary's Place': Mark Pender, Mike Spengler, Rich Rosenberg, Jerry Vivino, Ed Manion.

Songs:
'Lonesome Day', 'Into The Fire', 'Waitin' On A Sunny Day', 'Nothing Man', 'Counting On A Miracle', 'Empty

Sky', 'Worlds Apart', 'Let's Be Friends (Skin To Skin)', 'Further On (Up The Road)', 'The Fuse', 'Mary's Place', 'You're Missing', 'The Rising', 'Paradise', 'My City Of Ruins'.

Springsteen's decision to call in an 'outsider' to produce a new album, having depended on Jon Landau and Chuck Plotkin to perform the duties since 1975, was seen as a definite attempt to bring something new to the table. The result was a muscular rock album that was full of subtle instrumentation and sounds that had not been previously heard on a Bruce album. While the E Street Band were all present – with both Steve Van Zandt and Nils Lofgren carried over from the reunion tour – a number of other musicians were utilised, including a horn section for the superficially old-style Bruce party song, 'Mary's Place' (that nonetheless appears to be a man's attempt to celebrate a departed loved-one). 'Worlds Apart' featured a traditional Pakistani Qawwali group of singers and musicians, combining dramatically with the E Street Band's powerful rock on a song that appeals to people to "let love give what it gives". These 'foreign' voices emphasise the central message of the album that is understanding. The songs depict fear and despair, loss and pain, friendship and forgiveness. Whilst some songs were written prior to the terrorist attacks on the U.S.A. – 'Nothing Man', 'Further On (Up The Road)', 'My City Of Ruins' and others do not at first seem related to the album's themes – the sequencing and small details do allow the collection to flow and become a satisfying whole. The burning lust of 'The Fuse', for example, is described whilst in the background "down at the court house they're ringin' the flag down", suggesting a community mourning. 'My City Of Ruins', originally written for the economically battered Asbury Park, was immediately, and tragically, relevant to New York City as well – Bruce chose this to open the all-star telecast concert *A Tribute To Heroes*. Clear reactions to the events of September 11th were 'Into The Fire', 'Empty Sky' and the powerful 'Paradise' – a brave piece partially taking a suicide bomber's perspective. 'The Rising' was not a political call to arms, but importantly it was not a simple-minded condemnation of anyone. This was a thoughtful call to step back and understand all communities, not simply the victims and their survivors.

Highlights:

'Lonesome Day' – the strident violin opening to this song emphasised that Bruce was returning with a broader sonic palate. This song describes someone determined to over-come his loss – "find my way through this lonesome day".

'Empty Sky' – the pain and bitterness of someone who has suffered a great loss, this gives voice to the character's desire for "an eye for an eye", whilst the title's image can clearly be seen as a reference to the depleted Manhattan skyline after the terrorist attacks.

'My City Of Ruins' – written as a rallying call to the fading area of Asbury Park, the song was an apt end to an album that sought to find a peace and strength in commu-nity. The call of "come on, rise up" urged those in despair, such as the narrator of 'Empty Sky', to face the challenge of their losses, find a better day and "begin again".

Weak Spots:

'Countin' On A Miracle' – this is a somewhat histrionic piece and the inclusion of "fairytale" imagery feels forced. As with 'Lonesome Day', the character is determined to cope with his loss, but this feels stale with unoriginal lines such as "runnin' through the forest with the wolf at my heels".

Key Missing Tracks:

No outtakes have emerged as B-sides or bootlegs, although on the reunion and *The Rising* world tours, a handful of 'new' songs were played that didn't make the cut. It is unclear whether the Joe Grushecky co-writes 'Another Thin Line' and 'Code Of Silence' were recorded at *The Rising* sessions, but both received several plays towards the end of the 2000 leg of E Street Band touring and a live version of the latter emerged on the bonus disc of *The Essential*.

The Essential Bruce Springsteen, 2003.

Executive Producer:

Jon Landau.

Personnel:

Various.

Songs Disc One:

'Blinded By The Light', 'For You', 'Spirit In The Night', '4th Of July, Asbury Park (Sandy)', 'Rosalita (Come Out Tonight)', 'Thunder Road', 'Born To Run', 'Jungleland', 'Badlands', 'Darkness On The Edge Of Town', 'The

Promised Land', 'The River', 'Hungry Heart', 'Nebraska', 'Atlantic City'.

Songs Disc Two:
'Born In The U.S.A.', 'Glory Days', 'Dancing In The Dark', 'Tunnel Of Love', 'Brilliant Disguise', 'Human Touch', 'Lucky Town', 'Streets Of Philadelphia', 'The Ghost Of Tom Joad', 'The Rising', 'Mary's Place', 'Lonesome Day', 'American Skin (41 Shots)' (live), 'Land Of Hope And Dreams' (live).

Songs (Bonus Disc Three – all previously unreleased/non-album songs):
'From Small Things (Big Things One Day Come)', 'The Big Payback'#, 'Held Up Without A Gun' (live)★, 'Trapped' (live), 'None But The Brave', 'Missing'#, 'Lift Me Up'#, 'Viva Las Vegas'#, 'County Fair', 'Code Of Silence' (live), 'Dead Man Walkin''#, 'Countin' On A Miracle' (acoustic)★.
★ = alternate version of released song.
= previously released B-side, soundtrack or charity album track.

Eight and a half years after the *Greatest Hits* compilation, Sony persuaded Bruce and Jon Landau to compile a volume for the expanding *Essential* series. Joining the likes of Leonard Cohen and Bob Dylan, Bruce's collection was as generous as his legendary live shows. The series had set out with double-disc sets, but Springsteen assembled a bonus (limited edition) third disc for his effort, including a number of rare soundtrack and charity album performances, B-sides excluded from *Tracks* and unreleased live recordings. The fanatical Bruce fan would have forked out for the package with its well-illustrated booklet and fore-word by Bruce (also an unprecedented feature), but the third disc was a genuine 'bonus'. The introduction set out the concept of the album – seeking "to present a little of what each album has to offer" having seen "a lot of new faces" during recent touring. Bruce acknowledged that this may not satisfy the demands of old campaigners but, by penning this explanation, he headed off potential crit-icism.

Highlights:
The bonus disc collects a number of rare materials and a fascinating informal country blues take of a weaker rocker from *The Rising*, 'Countin' On A Miracle'.

Weak Spots:
The standard two disc edition closes with the two key elements of the *Live In New York City*, set in the shape of that album's previously unreleased songs, debuted live in 2000, 'American Skin (41 Shots)' and 'Land Of Hope And Dreams'. Perhaps these songs do work best live, but out of context – or rather in the context of an album of favourite studio recordings – they stand out for the change in atmosphere and for their length in the live arrangements. It was believed that the former song was recorded in the studio with radio plays in mind and new studio versions of both would have rounded off the album, at least more satisfying from a chronological point of view. Instead, after the trio of songs from *The Rising*, we are sent back two years to the Bruce world view pre-September 11th 2001. His message and concerns may not have changed but, as

with *Tracks*, the rules seem to have been bent here, to finally allow a glimpse of Bruce live at the very last, instead of adhering to a consistent line of only including studio efforts, in chronological order.

7. Blood Brothers (And Sisters)

Obviously, as an artist with such a large and dedicated fanbase, Bruce Springsteen is a desirable name to have on your album credits. Conversely, Bruce has no need to spread himself thinly and is notoriously careful over the use of his name. He has played numerous charity events, from the giant Amnesty 'Human Rights Now!' world tour with Sting, Peter Gabriel et al. in 1988, through to club gigs for local New Jersey causes such as the Patrick King Benefit for the murdered Long Branch policeman's family. However, if a promoter is hoping to attract Springsteen, a casual hint that he may be added to a bill has just the opposite effect – it becomes a certainty that he won't appear. Bruce doesn't like to be forced into situations, or for his name to be hijacked or misused. Thus, when it comes to appearing on records other than his own, Bruce needs to hear something in the music, or be a very close friend. Here are some of those select guest spots from Mr Springsteen.

Gary U.S. Bonds, *Dedication*, 1981; *On The Line*, 1982; *Back In 20*, 2004.
Born Gary Anderson, Gary U.S. Bonds became a star singing a rhythm and blues/soul repertoire, hitting it big with 'Quarter To Three', a song Bruce adopted for an encore for many shows in the 1970s. His star faded swiftly,

however, and by the late '70s he was a musical cast-off. Rock and roll aficionado Steve Van Zandt had been guest-leading the '60s group The Dovells when he first encountered Bonds in the 1970s. Having relinquished his role as producer and songwriter for Southside Johnny And The Asbury Jukes, Miami Steve took the opportunity provided by a gap in the E Street Band tour in 1980 to produce in his favoured rhythm and blues vein again. The resulting Bonds album, *Dedication*, featured appearances from the entire E Street Band and three exclusive (still unreleased by the writer) Springsteen songs – 'This Little Girl', 'Your Love' and 'Dedication'. Written in the Bonds style, they were additionally produced by Bruce. Released by EMI, the album and a couple of singles from it were minor hits and the following year the formula was repeated. This time, Bruce contributed seven of the album *On The Line*'s songs – 'Hold On (To What You Got)', 'Out Of Work', 'Club Soul City', 'Love's On The Line', 'Rendezvous', 'Angelyne' and 'All I Need'. So while Bruce's own album of 1982 was a downbeat acoustic masterpiece, a parallel fun rock record featuring the E Street Band and Springsteen songs could still be found. (Both albums were reissued on a double CD package in 2004.)

The success of the two records Miami Steve and Bruce produced was not sufficient to sustain Bond's career as a major attraction for long and he subsequently returned to playing the oldies circuit and small club dates. In 2004, however, he had another shot at success with a comeback album archly entitled *Back In 20*, for which Bruce separately recorded a guitar and backing vocal (the wonders of technology) that was added to the song 'Can't Teach An Old Dog New Tricks', also featuring Southside Johnny.

Joe Ely, *Letter To Laredo*, 1995.
Native of Texas, and sometime Flatlander alongside Butch Hancock and Jimmie Dale Gilmore, Ely is a highly accomplished country singer-songwriter, with strong Mexican/cowboy slants to his recordings. His 1995 album, *Letter To Laredo*, is full of Spanish guitar flourishes and driving rhythm, and features Bruce on passionate backing vocals on both the opening track 'All Just To Get To You' and the closer, 'I'm A Thousand Miles From Home'.

Joe Grushecky, *American Babylon*, 1995; *Coming Home*, 1997; *Down The Road Apiece* (live), 1999.
Having stoked the fires of his fans' imaginations by reuniting the E Street Band for his first *Greatest Hits* package in early 1995, Bruce then confounded the inevitably renewed interest by turning his attention away from his own career to help out a friend, Pittsburgh rocker and sometime teacher, Joe Grushecky, leader of the Houserockers. Grushecky's wife apparently suggested that he ask Bruce to play on a new record. Eventually their collaboration resulted in *American Babylon*, a rare example of Bruce taking the producer's role and the first time since he and Steve Van Zandt had worked on Gary U.S. Bonds' comeback albums in the early 1980s. Bruce described the project as "a record made very quickly over a long period of time", with its roots back prior to 'Streets Of Philadelphia'. Springsteen ironically produced all but the title track and contributes much muscular playing on a variety of instruments and some telling background vocal moments. The sound is very akin to late-period Bruce, as are the lyrical themes (not just the Springsteen-penned 'Dark And Bloody Ground' and the co-write with

Grushecky, 'Homestead') and the album could easily pass as a solid, but not classic, Springsteen record, had he taken all the vocal duties. Instead, Grushecky does a very fine job, with his tight band and its special guest. Also helping out are Patti Scialfa with a strong vocal on 'Comin' Down Maria', and Bruce's sister Pam, who took the cover photography, while there are a couple of appearances of two members of Bruce's 1992–3 touring band, Zack Alford and Shayne Fontaine, subbing for various Houserockers. In support of the album's release, Bruce undertook a small club tour with Grushecky (who had given up his day job for this crack at success in his 40s) and his band, bringing in much media attention for Bruce's protégé, with Springsteen appearing on the live B-sides to 'Labour Of Love' taken from *American Babylon*.

Two years on from the first serious collaboration between Springsteen and Grushecky, the Houserockers returned with *Coming Home*. This time around, Bruce's contribution was restricted to co-writing three songs; 'I'm Not Sleeping', 'Idiot's Delight' and the particularly striking war-survivor's tale, '1945', propelled by a beautiful gentle shuffle. The album was another fine effort, but the attention given to *American Babylon* had not translated into sales and *Coming Home* won no new fans. *Down The Road Apiece* was a live collection that featured Bruce on four songs from the earlier club tour and a Houserockers' performance of his 'Light Of Day', a track Grushecky and his band would later record twice – for the tribute albums *One Step Up/Two Steps Back* (rocking out) and *Light Of Day: A Tribute To Bruce Springsteen* (a countrified take).

Joe Grushecky's current manager, Bob Benjamin, has organised an annual charity evening of music named after

Bruce's 'Light Of Day', with proceeds going to The Parkinson's Disease Foundation (Benjamin suffers from the illness). Grushecky has played at these concert events, with Bruce turning up as an unbilled 'surprise' guest at each one to date. Grushecky continues to make records and plays regularly in his native Pittsburgh – although he has resumed teaching commitments with stardom proving too elusive. He notes on his website his pleasure at Bruce's inclusion of a 1999 live rendition of 'Code Of Silence', a previously unreleased co-write from 1997, on the bonus disc of *The Essential* collection.

John Wesley Harding, *Awake*, 1994.

This fine, under-appreciated, eclectic singer-songwriter, with a cutting wit and great melodies has, on occasion, stripped back his power-pop side to reveal a considerable folk influence (notably recording an album, *Trad Arr. Jones*, based on the work of English folk singer Nic Jones). *Awake* saw Harding roots-rocking in his own style with a new backing band he dubbed the Gangsta Folk. At the album sessions he recorded a version of 'Jackson Cage' for the charity Bruce tribute album, *One Step Up/Two Steps Back*. The 2000 reissue of *Awake* features both this effective cover and a live duet with Bruce (from June 1994) of another song from *The River*, 'Wreck On The Highway'. In 1995, John Wesley Harding joined a small list of artists who have opened for Bruce in concerts over the years when he was approached to do the early *Tom Joad* shows. Perhaps Bruce was initially uncertain how an audience would react to him standing alone on stage for a whole night. Very swiftly, however, it became apparent that Bruce remained an immensely commanding stage presence, unplugged and solo, and he dispensed with an opening act. Harding was also present at the Ani DiFranco-arranged Woody Guthrie tribute in 1996, in which Bruce participated.

Emmylou Harris, *Red Dirt Girl*, 2000.
One of the most distinctive vocalists of all time, the country music giant that is Emmylou Harris had, in 1995, revived a career that had lost focus when the major record labels became more interested in the glossy side of Nashville. Harris had turned to Daniel Lanois, U2 producer and restorer of Bob Dylan, for critical attention to her 1989 album, *Oh Mercy*. Lanois has a distinctive style of adding mysterious soundscapes and textures to the backing tracks he works on and he selected a great collection of covers for Harris' *Wrecking Ball*. In 1999, Harris teamed up with old friend Linda Ronstadt for a duet album, *The Tucson Sessions*. This record featured the first major artist cover of a Patti Scialfa song in their version of 'Valerie', and closed out with Bruce's 'Across The Border'. The belated solo follow-up album saw Harris use Malcolm Burn, responsible for recording *Wrecking Ball* and of similar aural sensibilities to Lanois, as producer. This time Harris wrote or co-wrote all but one song. However, professing herself a big fan of Patti Scialfa's debut album *Rumble Doll*, which she felt had been neglected, she wanted to use Patti's voice on this personal album and asked her to duet on the song 'Tragedy' – she obliged and brought Bruce along to add backing vocals. At her Albert Hall concert on the subsequent world tour, Harris played *Rumble Doll* in its entirety before her own set!

Jerry Lee Lewis, *The Pilgrim*, 2005.
The 'killer' asked a variety of rock music's elder statesmen to contribute duet vocals to his new album and plenty of big names agreed. Along with Mick Jagger, Rod Stewart and Eric Clapton, Bruce makes an appearance with a new version of his 'Pink Cadillac'.

Johnny Lyon – Southside Johnny And The Asbury Jukes, *Better Days*, 1993.
An old Jersey scene bandmate of Bruce, Southside Johnny and his rhythm and blues band signed to Epic and threatened to make it as big as their New Jersey friend. Their debut, *I Don't Want To Go Home* was released in 1976, produced by Steve Van Zandt (as were the next two) and featured the exclusive Bruce-penned songs 'The Fever' and 'You Mean So Much To Me'. The second album, *This Time It's For Real* contained three Van Zandt and Springsteen co-writes, 'Little Girl So Fine', 'Love On The Wrong Side Of Town' and 'When You Dance'. *Hearts Of Stone* was the last Southside album to include exclusive Springsteen material for many years, with the title track 'Talk To Me' and the co-write (with Steve and Southside) 'Trapped Again'. A comeback album, *Better Days*, in 1991, again produced by Little Steven, included a nostalgic Van Zandt song, 'It's Been A Long Time' that featured Southside, Steve and Bruce trading lines. The album also contained a new Bruce effort, 'All The Way Home', on which he played.

Jesse Malin, *Messed Up Here Tonight* (live), 2004.
Ryan Adams, whose own solo debut brought comparisons to Bob Dylan, produced Jesse Malin's first album. Ironically,

the resulting release was reviewed as a Springsteen-influenced piece of work, a tag that Malin was obviously comfortable with, admitting his admiration for Bruce and contributing a cover of 'Hungry Heart' to a tribute album. In 2003, Malin appeared at charity Christmas concerts organised by Bruce associates and featuring the man himself. A performance of Bruce duetting on Malin's 'Wendy' (interestingly, the female character's name in 'Born To Run') was taken from these shows for this self-released compilation of live tracks and rarities.

Marah, *Float Away With The Friday Night Gods*, 2002.
A Philadelphia-based rock band, often compared to Springsteen, Marah were signed by Steve Earle to his Artemis label for their second album. This gained them much critical praise including being U.K. magazine *Uncut*'s album of the month. Their third album featured an undistinguished guitar and vocal contribution from Bruce on the title cut but the record failed to deliver on their promise, with poor sales following.

Mike Ness, *Cheating At Solitaire*, 1999.
On this solo album from the former singer with the punk band Social Distortion, Bruce turns up for an unspectacular vocal duet on 'Misery Loves Company'.

Roy Orbison, *A Black And White Night* (live), 1988.
Name-checked in 'Thunder Road', Springsteen admitted in his *Greatest Hits* sleevenotes that he consciously tried to steal Roy Orbison's vocal style for the song. Years later, in 1987, Bruce joined a star-studded group of musicians, including Elvis Costello, Jackson Browne and (incongru-

ously) the gruff Tom Waits to form a unique backing band for the big-voiced Big O. The show was filmed in black and white for both television broadcast and commercial release and captured Orbison on top form, coming as it did in the midst of a last-minute career renaissance. Orbison also enjoyed membership of the Traveling Wilburys supergroup, alongside Bob Dylan, George Harrison, Tom Petty and Jeff Lynne, and recorded the hit solo album *Mystery Girl* shortly before his death.

John Prine, *The Missing Years*, 1991.
During Bruce's prolonged recording sessions in the years between *Tunnel Of Love* and his 1992 albums, John Prine employed Springsteen's talents for a backing vocal on 'Take A Look At My Heart' on his own comeback album of 1991. The Grammy-winning Contemporary Folk album featured a harder sound than much of Prine's other witty and satirical but largely acoustic-based work, courtesy of members of Tom Petty's Heartbreakers. Bruce's involvement is curiously inconsequential, however.

Lou Reed, *Street Hassle*, 1978.
Apparently recording in the same studio complex as were both Springsteen and Patti Smith, Reed wanted a second voice for a spoken word segment to his epic song 'Street Hassle', the title track to his in-progress album, and he approached Steve Van Zandt to ask Bruce. In his recent compilation, *NYC Man*, Reed bemoans the fact that while Springsteen agreed to record the part, he did not allow his name to be used in the credits, thus failing to attract more of Bruce's fans over to the ex-Velvet Underground man's work.

In the legendary 1978 live rant/album *Take No Prisoners*, and half way through his bona-fide solo hit 'Walk On The Wild Side', Lou digresses, as he does for much of the album, this time to defend Bruce: "Springsteen is alright, by the way. He gets my seal of approval – I think he's groovy." Reed then takes the opportunity to launch his infamous attack on rock critics, at first in relation to how they had turned on Bruce in his view and very swiftly on to their attitudes in general...

Curiously, the infamously independent Lou Reed established a brief songwriting partnership with future E Streeter Nils Lofgren in the late 1970s. Put into contact by mutual producer Bob Ezrin, the two songwriters completed a set of songs (largely with Reed providing lyrics and Lofgren the music) by postal exchanges!

Warren Zevon, *The Wind*, 2003.

A singer-songwriter who specialised in a cutting wit in his lyrics, Warren Zevon included 'Jeannie Needs A Shooter' on his 1980 album *Bad Luck Streak At Dancing School*, credited as a collaboration with Springsteen, although this was apparently written in the early '70s by Bruce and largely re-written by Zevon. After a few patchy years, Zevon's albums *Life'll Kill Ya* and *My Ride's Here* returned him to critical acclaim, although the determination to make a mark makes them sound a little self-conscious. However, in 2002, he was given the news that recent health worries were actually the result of inoperable lung cancer. Vowing to make the most of whatever time he had left, Zevon worked on what he knew to be his last album, *The Wind*. He actually outlived expectations and saw the 2003 release of the record – eventually succumbing to the disease within a week of it charting. Bruce Springsteen was one of the many friends who lined up to give Warren a hand on the record. Whilst being very much a Zevon piece of work, Bruce's contributions were telling. A documentary made at the time of the sessions (released on DVD as *(Inside) Out: Warren Zevon*, 2004) reveals Bruce bolstering Zevon's weakened vocals on 'Disorder In The House' and adding a stinging guitar solo that clearly impresses the song's author. Springsteen also helps out with vocals on 'Prison Grove'. In 2004, the late Zevon, together with Bruce, won the Grammy for Best Rock Performance By A Duo Or Group With Vocal for 'Disorder In The House' and *The Wind* also won the somewhat strange award for Best Contemporary Folk Album.

8. Paying Tribute

In addition to lending his guitar or vocal talents to others' recordings, Bruce Springsteen has donated exclusive recordings and performances to a number of charity and tribute albums. With an acclaimed recording career spanning more than three decades, there have also been a number of tribute albums dedicated to Bruce himself. The more significant of these collections are detailed as follows:

CHARITY ALBUMS FEATURING EXCLUSIVE BRUCE SPRINGSTEEN RECORDINGS:

No Nukes: The MUSE Concerts, 1979.

Bruce's first overtly political statement was his participation in these anti-nuclear weapon benefit concerts. The regular E Street Band concert closer of 'Devil With The Blue Dress Medley' was included on the double album, along with a Bruce and Jackson Browne duet of 'Stay'.

We Are The World: U.S.A. For Africa, 1985.

Bruce sang as part of the massed choir of superstars on 'We Are The World', and contributed an impressive live cover of Jimmy Cliff's 'Trapped', an alternative version of which appeared on the bonus disc of *Essential*.

For Our Children, 1989.

A charity album to benefit children affected by HIV/AIDS. This collected original performances of children's songs recorded by established artists, including Bruce's take on 'Chicken Hips And Lizard Lips' and Bob Dylan singing 'This Old Man'.

The Concert For The Rock And Roll Hall Of Fame, 1995.

As part of the brief reunion of Bruce and his band, the E Streeters were recruited as a house band, along with Booker T. and the MGs, for the concert inauguration of the Rock And Roll Hall Of Fame Museum in Cleveland, Ohio. Playing back-up to both Jerry Lee Lewis and Chuck Berry, Bruce and his band also played a brief set that included an intense rendition of 'Hey Bo Diddley' that evolved into their own 'She's The One'. A highlight for the image, if not musically, was Bruce performing a duet with Bob Dylan on the latter's 'Forever Young'. The subsequent album featured three E Street performances – 'Shake, Rattle And Roll' and, with Jerry Lee Lewis, 'Great Balls Of Fire' and 'Whole Lotta Shakin' Goin' On'. Proceeds from the album went to the Museum.

TRIBUTE ALBUMS FEATURING EXCLUSIVE BRUCE SPRINGSTEEN RECORDINGS:

Johnny Cash, *Kindred Spirits: A Tribute To The Songs Of Johnny Cash*, 2002.
Bob Dylan, Steve Earle and Emmylou Harris were among those paying homage to the then ailing Cash. Springsteen's fine contribution of 'Give My Love To Rose' was taken from his satellite link performance at a 1999 tribute concert.

Harry Chapin, *The Tribute Concert*, 1987.
Classic songwriter Harry Chapin, who scored a number one single with the classic 'Cat's In The Cradle', co-written with his wife, died in a car accident in 1981. An occasional acquaintance, Bruce was asked to perform at a 1987 tribute concert and his thoughtful rendition of Chapin's 'Remember When The Music' was included on the subsequent album.

Woody Guthrie, *Folkways: A Vision Shared: A Tribute To Woody Guthrie And Leadbelly*, 1988.
1988 may have seen Bruce on his Tunnel Of Love Express World Tour, but his recordings of 'I Ain't Got No Home' and 'Vigilante Man', featuring abbreviated formations of the E Street Band, were rootsy highlights of this project. Both Springsteen selections were from Guthrie's reper-toire, the former handled in a very simple acoustic arrangement with Bruce, Nils Lofgren and Roy Bittan whose organ deliberately sounds like a more traditional accordion. For 'Vigilante Man', Max Weinberg's heart-beat drumming and Lofgren's occasional slide guitar drive a

subtly rocking take. The album's cause was the preservation of the Folkways and Woody Guthrie catalogues and archives with proceeds from the album aiding The Smithsonian Institute's purchase of these. Fellow artists recruited to the album included U2, Emmylou Harris and, sounding particularly engaged and happy with just an acoustic guitar, Bob Dylan performing 'Pretty Boy Floyd', a precursor to his wonderful early nineties brace of solo traditional albums.

Woody Guthrie, *'Til We Outnumber 'Em: The Songs Of Woody Guthrie*, 2000.
Woody's profile had been raised considerably by the critically acclaimed Billy Bragg and Wilco *Mermaid Avenue* collaborations. Preserving the Woody Guthrie Archives is, however, an ongoing expensive business and thus, Ani DiFranco gathered an impressive group to perform Woody's songs at a concert to benefit the Archives and the Rock And Roll Hall Of Fame Museum's education projects. Alongside Bruce were Billy Bragg, Ramblin' Jack Elliott and Arlo Guthrie. As with the previous Guthrie tribute album he had participated in, Springsteen had two performances – 'Riding In My Car' and 'Plane Wreck At Los Gatos (Deportee)' – included on the final record. The album was painstakingly assembled by DiFranco and her Righteous Babe label against the problems of dealing with so many different record companies, emerging some three years after the event.

Curtis Mayfield, *A Tribute To Curtis Mayfield*, 1994.
Bruce contributes a mysterious take on 'Gypsy Woman', produced in collaboration with Tommy Sims. Under-

pinned by a very prominent bass and featuring a number of percussive flourishes – all presumably supplied by Sims – this has a very untypical Bruce sound in relation to the official canon of released studio albums, although the slow pace and restrained vocal were revealed to be a common style during the 'lost' 1990s, as evidenced by *Tracks*.

Elvis Presley, *The Last Temptation Of Elvis*, 1990.
A charity (for Nordoff–Robbins Music Therapy) tribute album to the King, compiled by the U.K. weekly music paper *New Musical Express (N.M.E.)*. Big hitters featured on the album included Paul McCartney, Robert Plant and The Pogues, with Bruce contributing a storming take on 'Viva Las Vegas'. Jeff Porcaro and Ian McLagan took the drum and keyboard parts, while Bob Ludwig, long-time behind-the-scenes man, responsible for mastering Bruce's records, played bass on the recording, as noted in the cut's inclusion on *The Essential* bonus disc.

Pete Seeger, *Where Have All The Flowers Gone: The Songs Of Pete Seeger*, 1998.
Recorded in November 1997, Springsteen utilised the talents of ten additional musicians on the song Pete Seeger had made his own in the politicised folk world of the 1960s, 'We Shall Overcome'. This large band included an accordionist, a couple of Asbury Jukes (Rich Rosenberg and Ed Manion), Patti Scialfa and Soozie Tyrell. The latter pair provide expansive backing vocals and the overall effect is hymnal – even, appropriately considering the time of year it was recorded, carol-like – as Bruce's shuffling take on the anthem of defiance offers a more reflective interpretation.

Warren Zevon, *Enjoy Every Sandwich: The Songs Of Warren Zevon*, 2004.

Springsteen and Zevon had been comrades through the years and Bruce gave a helping hand to Warren's final album, *The Wind*. This tribute album compiled original recordings along with recent live takes from Bob Dylan and Bruce's version of 'My Ride's Here', performed in concert after the announcement that Zevon had finally succumbed to his lung cancer in 2003.

TRIBUTE ALBUMS TO BRUCE SPRINGSTEEN:

The Bruce Springsteen Songbook, 1996.

The Connoisseur label produced a number of compilation albums consisting of covers of an artist's songs, rather than being actual tribute projects. However, whilst the selections were by their nature previously released and not exclusively recorded, the *Songbook* series did make available again some hard-to-find songs in a convenient collection. For the Bruce volume, Warren Zevon's recording of 'Jeannie Needs A Shooter' – still unreleased in any form by the writer – and a couple of unlikely covers by U.K. acts Frankie Goes To Hollywood ('Born To Run') and Everything But The Girl ('Tougher Than The Rest') are of particular interest. (NB The featured Little River Band track 'Light Of Day' is NOT the Bruce song!)

One Step Up/Two Steps Back, 1997.

This double-disc tribute album was split into a disc of all-new covers by friends and admirers, such as Nils Lofgren tackling 'Wreck On The Highway', Joe Grushecky rocking out on 'Light Of Day' and Ben E. King's measured '4th Of July, Asbury Park (Sandy)'. The other disc contained covers selected from older projects, such as Southside Johnny's original take on 'The Fever' and David Bowie's 1975 recording of 'It's Hard To Be A Saint In The City', featuring Roy Bittan. (Bowie also recorded 'Growin' Up' at this time for *Station To Station*, although neither track made the final album.) Released on the tiny Right Stuff label, the package is thoughtfully produced with all the artists (including those whose recordings were done some twenty-odd years previously) contributing brief notes regarding their appreciation of Springsteen's writing. Band details are given and the cover art features the boardwalk at Asbury Park. Some proceeds of the sales were donated to the World Hunger Year charity. (NB The album was later sold as two separate CDs.)

Badlands: A Tribute To Bruce Springsteen's Nebraska, 2000.

Although originally released in the U.S. on the indie label Sub Pop, Warner Music picked up the rights for its wider distribution, presumably impressed by the quality of the artists involved. Chrissie Hynde contributes a dreamy, haunted version of the original album's title track and, elsewhere, all the recordings are significantly different to Bruce's own stark acoustic versions. This emphasises how strongly constructed the lyrics actually are, in that they bear up to such a variety of styles and voices (half are sung by women). E Street Band concert renditions from the *Live 1975–85* box, and the recent reunion tours, also indicate that, given time, band arrangements could have resulted in an equally strong – but clearly different – album to the solo masterpiece that was eventually released. Of extra interest on this unusual tribute (the album was hardly the global commercial hit that Carole King's *Tapestry* or Fleetwood Mac's *Rumours*, other albums given special tributes, proved to be) is the inclusion of covers of three *Nebraska* outtakes. Johnny Cash, who had already released an album called *Johnny 99* featuring both that song and 'Highway Patrolman', cut 'I'm On Fire' with a slowed-up version of his Sun-era backing sound. The Mavericks' Raul Malo sings a restrained 'Downbound Train' and the interesting Damien Jurado and Rose Thomas add a duet of 'Wages Of Sin' that is disappointingly close to Bruce's own rendition, as released on *Tracks*.

Born To Run 2003: The Best Of The Boss, 2003.

The U.K.-based music and movie magazine, *Uncut*, successfully established itself in a tough market in 1997, and helped cement its place by standing out from rivals with the offer of a free compilation CD with every issue. These CDs are often thematic, compiled by a guest artist, or assembled as a tribute to an act featured in the month's issue. Having previously graced the cover in December 2000, and on the September 2002 issue, which included an eighteen-page feature surrounding the release of *The Rising*, Bruce was back in April 2003. This time there were two alternative cover pictures – Bruce in the late 1970s, or in mid-1980s pomp. The multiple-issue idea has been used to entice collectors of all things Beatles by various publications, but in the case of Bruce, *Uncut* was offering two different and exclusive cover compilations as well, giving more incentive to those considering buying both editions. Many of the featured tracks had previously been available on the contributing artist's studio albums or as B-sides (some as reissue bonuses), but having them brought together was a treat for Bruce fans, whilst major artists such as The Waterboys ('Independence Day'), Badly Drawn Boy ('Thunder Road') and Jesse Malin ('Hungry Heart') contributed exclusive new recordings. These are certainly worth getting hold of in second-hand stores.

Light Of Day: A Tribute To Bruce Springsteen, 2003.

A double-disc set, put together to aid the charities The Parkinson's Disease Foundation and The Kristen Ann Carr Fund; Joe Grushecky's manager Bob Benjamin initiated this project. Elliott Murphy compiled and co-ordinated the release, whilst Dave Marsh supplied a foreword. Nils Lofgren, Dan Bern and Matthew Ryan all contributed, whilst Billy Bragg's cover of 'Mansion On The Hill' is accompanied by a quote from the Englishman – "Springsteen makes me keep my faith in America". (In some territories a third disc, featuring little-known acts, was included.)

9. Proving It All Night

When Bruce Springsteen announced the forthcoming release of the *Tracks* boxset in 1998, he also declared his intention to embark on an accompanying tour and added that, "everyone will be happy with my choice of band". This alluded to the mixed reaction he had received for his undoubtedly competent but nonetheless somewhat anonymous gang of session players with whom he toured the world during 1992–1993. There is a perceptible thrill at the start of a Springsteen concert when the lights have dimmed and one by one the Big Man, Miami Steve, the Phantom, the Professor et al. climb onto the stage, before Bruce himself arrives to kick off another magical night. There are very few acts where the audience is quite so genuinely excited to see the keyboard or bass player arrive, emphasising as it does the shared history of the band with their leader (OK, their 'Boss' as he has been dubbed by the media since the 1980s, presumably for his leadership on stage) and the audience. Each band member has been there for hundreds of legendary nights, been there when those classic songs were laid down in the studio, and here they are, where they have surely always belonged, along-side their friend Bruce Springsteen, on stage, before your eyes. When Springsteen penned 'Blood Brothers', the song that both gave the documentary of the brief 1995 reunion its name and obliquely described the band's relationship, he sounded uncertain about this possibly retrograde move. Having disbanded his group officially in 1989 to try out new sounds and musical ideas, Bruce was anxious as to whether "I've lost or I've gained sight" with the experience. It took a while for him to finally conclude (or, perhaps, admit) that what makes his music so distinguished is the element of community both in the lyrics and amongst the long-term friends of the E Street Band that help him deliver them with such conviction.

Following are brief career 'biographies' of the musicians who have comprised the E Street Band, detailing these popular but often overlooked figures' own musical lives in addition to their work with Springsteen. Additionally, there are summaries of other key figures crucial to Bruce Springsteen's music during his extensive rock and roll career. (Where available, official websites are listed after the entry, as are the birthdays of current E Street Band members.)

Mike Appel

With Bruce: manager, producer, (background vocals on 'Thunder Road'). 1972–1976.

According to Dave Marsh, the rock journalist and Bruce insider (his wife is Barbara Carr of Jon Landau Management) who has been the semi-official biographer of the artist, Mike Appel got Bruce to sign his first contract to Appel's Laurel Canyon company "in the unlighted parking lot of a bar". New Jersey native and surfboard maker Carl 'Tinker' West had performed management duties in the days of Steel Mill, but had pointed the budding solo artist Springsteen in the direction of Appel who was initially impressed but non-committal. After a chastening experience in California, Bruce returned to the comforting familiarity of Jersey where he had friends and a reputation as the area's hottest guitarist, and he renewed contact with Appel, who this time snatched at the chance to sign him. The parking lot story has, of course, been contested by Appel, but the image of Bruce's first professional manager as a somewhat shady, pushy opportunist has gone down in rock folklore. Appel was indeed pushy, by his own admission, and his doggedness helped gain Bruce his audition with Columbia's John Hammond and, later on, his aggressive plugging got Bruce invaluable radio plays that helped to spread the word beyond the boundaries of Jersey. Mike Appel's background was not the rock and roll that Springsteen was immersed in, tellingly, cutting his music business teeth as a staff writer for the bubblegum-pop Wes Farrell Organisation, helping to pen advertising jingles and songs for the Partridge Family. 'I Can Feel Your Heartbeat', 'Somebody Wants To Love You', 'Umbrella Man', 'Rainmaker' and 'Doesn't Somebody Want To Be Wanted' – a Top Ten hit – were all credited to Farrell, Appel and Jim Cretecos. It was with the latter that he sought to break away from this transient pop and move into music that was more likely to last and sustain a career. An early attempt was producing an album by a metal act named Sir Lord Baltimore. It was not a happy experience. Appel and Cretecos would, however, establish Laurel Canyon Limited for production and publishing, and go on to manage Bruce Springsteen and produce his first two albums.

After the acrimonious split with Springsteen, Mike Appel would never have another shot at the big time. To raise money in the early 1980s, Appel sold Bruce his share of publishing and production and, in 1986, made 'peace' with Springsteen after meeting for a meal. Watching Bruce's success from a distance, he has interestingly stated in interviews that he does not much care for the music with which Bruce has become a megastar – surely justification of Bruce's decision to be rid of him. Whilst trying to sound sanguine about the affair, Appel clearly feels that Jon Landau is to blame for his loss of control of Springsteen. In 1992, Marc Eliot's *Down Thunder Road: The Making Of Bruce Springsteen* was published. Credited as having "the participation" of Appel, the book is essentially the ex-manager's side of the story. Amongst a mass of legal documents are sideswipes at the way Springsteen held firm against Appel's ideas of playing larger venues, of selling official merchandise and of issuing a live album post-*Born To Run*, but one-by-one agreed to do all of these ventures for Jon Landau. The implication is that Landau is a dark manipulator and Appel just a naïve idealist. His previous and subsequent career would suggest that, while he was key to Bruce's finding his way into the business, Mike Appel did not have the ability to turn him into the artist he would become.

(In the 1998 dispute between Bruce and Masquerade Music over the release of a number of early songs on the albums 'Prodigal Son' and 'Before The Fame', Appel testified on Bruce's behalf in court, an ironic situation that saw the pair briefly reunited in London. The defence claimed that Jim Cretecos still held rights to the recordings and had sold them on legally. Bruce won the case.)

Roy 'Professor' Bittan (b. 2 July 1949)

With Bruce: piano, organ, electric piano, glockenspiel. 1974–present.

Roy Bittan entered into Bruce-world when he auditioned to replace the departing David Sancious in the E Street Band during the *Born To Run* sessions, having previously worked on Broadway musicals. Danny Federici (who held the veto as the band's incumbent keyboardist and who would therefore have to work most closely with the new recruit) liked what he saw and gave him the thumbs up. As a session player, Bittan was much in demand and he recorded with David Bowie in 1975, the sessions including Bowie's covers of 'Growin' Up' and 'It's Hard To Be A Saint In The City', and with Dire Straits (including the suspiciously 'Jungleland'-like 'Carousel Waltz' opening to 'Tunnel Of Love' on *Making Movies*). Meat Loaf called on his services on the operatic *Bat Out Of Hell* album and beyond, while there's a fine Bittan performance on 'Finish Line' on the neglected 1996 Lou Reed album *Set The Twilight Reeling*.

Over the years, Bittan has undertaken occasional production work in addition to his session playing, helming projects for Chicago, Catie Curtis and Celine Dion, and rescuing the protracted sessions for Lucinda Williams' comeback album *Car Wheels On A Gravel Road* that eventually emerged in 1998. This was the follow-up to her acclaimed 1992 release *Sweet Old World* and was originally in the hands of Steve Earle and Ray Kennedy before they walked away, apparently frustrated by Williams' extreme perfectionism and procrastination. Upon its release, *Car Wheels* was critically lauded as a masterpiece, garnering many important awards, including the Grammy for Contemporary Folk Album.

Despite being a relative newcomer to Bruce's band (compared with old comrades and friends like Federici and Tallent), Roy Bittan's professionalism seemed to be a reassuring rock for Springsteen once he made the momentous decision to disband his E Street comrades and record with a new group of musicians in 1989. Indeed, Bruce credited Roy for kick-starting his recording in the 1990s, after he had spent some time concentrating on domestic matters with Patti Scialfa. The keyboardist had written some instrumentals that Bruce liked enough to develop into the fully-fledged songs 'Roll Of The Dice' and 'Real World' that would emerge on 1992's *Human Touch*, the first time Bruce had shared songwriting credits on a studio album. Bittan was also listed as a co-producer on this album (that ironically also featured his E Street predecessor David Sancious) and given an additional production credit for *Lucky Town*. He would be the cornerstone of the controversial – because it wasn't the E Street Band! – group that backed Bruce on his extensive 1992–93 tour. Bittan also worked on Patti Scialfa's *Rumble Doll* and was reunited with his E Street Band colleagues for the 1999 world tour.

Ernest 'Boom' Carter

With Bruce: drums. 1974.

Ernest Carter landed a spot in the formative E Street Band when Vini Lopez's musical and, more urgently, behavioural shortcomings had become too much of a liability. With live performances already booked when the decision to replace Lopez had been made, in February 1974, keyboard player David Sancious suggested his friend Carter who was swiftly accepted. Carter's tenure with the band lasted just under six months, before he and Sancious departed to form their own band, Tone (see Sancious' entry). During the 1970s, Carter also made appearances on recordings by Southside Johnny and Steve Forbert, amongst others, before he joined the band the Fairlanes the following decade. Bruce Springsteen made a guest live appearance with this band in 1987, the year of their *Hit The Road* album, but left after they put out *All The Way Live* in 1990. Since then, he has released a solo album, worked with Clarence Clemons, Bonnie Raitt and Howard Tate and, most recently, played on the J.C. Flyer album *Movin' On*, 2004.

Album:
Temple Of Boom, 2001.
(See David Sancious for Tone releases.)

Clarence 'Big Man' Clemons
(b. 11 January 1942)

With Bruce: saxophone, percussion, background vocals. 1972–89, 1995, 1999–present.

Clarence's entry into the E Street Band was immortalised in the *Born To Run* track 'Tenth Avenue Freeze-Out' – "the Big Man joined the band... [and] all the little pretties raise their hands". Although he played little part on the first Springsteen album, his importance swiftly grew both on record (with 1975's 'Jungleland' a highlight) and as Bruce's sideman in concerts.

In 1977, he was cast as a trumpet player in Martin Scorsese's film *New York, New York* alongside Robert De Niro, launching an intermittent acting career that has included narrating an episode of *The Simpsons* and a role in *Blues Brothers 2000*. In the early 1980s, he began a solo career in addition to his extensive session work. A duet with Jackson Browne, 'You've Got A Friend' was a minor hit, whilst his albums featured a couple of exclusive Springsteen donations in 'Savin' Up' and 'Summer On Signal Hill'. After the E Street Band broke up, Clemons toured both with his own band the Red Bank Rockers and Ringo Starr's All Starr troupe, as well as briefly running his own New Jersey club. Clarence was present and correct for the 1999–2000 reunion and *The Rising* album and tour, whilst fitting in gigs with his new band, the Temple Of Soul.

Albums:
Rescue, 1983
The Chief, 1983
Hero, 1985
A Night With Mr. C, 1989
Peacemaker, 1995
Get It On, (Aja And The Big Man), 1997
Live In Asbury Park, (with Temple Of Soul), 2002
Live In Asbury Park Vol. II, (with Temple Of Soul), 2004
Website: www.clarenceclemons.com

Jim Cretecos

With Bruce: assistant manager, producer. 1972–74.
   Jim Cretecos was effectively the junior partner to Mike

Appel in the management team of Bruce Springsteen's first years as a Columbia recording artist, before quitting in 1974, frustrated by their financial position. Since their split, Cretecos' most prominent role was as the source of the early recordings sold on as 'Before The Fame' and 'Prodigal Son' – material for which the offending small labels claimed they had bought the rights to. Bruce successfully went to court to prevent their distribution.

Danny Federici (b. 23 January 1950)

With Bruce: accordion, organ, glockenspiel, piano, vox continental, farfisa, background vocals. Pre-contract, 1972–1989, 1995, 1999–present.

A member both of Child and Steel Mill, Federici was already a long-time associate of Springsteen when he came to record his first album in 1973. Thus, it was Federici who had the job of approving a replacement for David Sancious as the second keyboardist in the band and his choice of Roy Bittan proved a great success. Unlike the other band members, Federici has not devoted himself to session work, although he has worked with Joan Armatrading and Graham Parker amongst others.

An enthusiast of the accordion, Federici's solo albums have been instrumental smooth jazz affairs, with Nils Lofgren and Garry Tallent helping out on his debut.

Albums:
Flemington, 1997
Danny Federici, (expanded reissue of *Flemington*), 2001
Sweet, 2004

Suki Lahav

With Bruce: violin, background vocals. 1974–75.

Suki Lahav's involvement with Springsteen was brief and fortuitous. The wife of Louis Lahav, engineer on *The Wild, The Innocent And The E Street Shuffle*, was working on the new Springsteen album when Bruce required strings for some of the tracks and Suki happened to be a violinist. Her playing stands out on the epic 'Jungleland' and she was employed for a handful of concerts at the time with a live cover of Bob Dylan's 'I Want You' regarded as an E Street Band highlight of the period. In 1975, the Lahavs headed off to Israel (with a suggestion that Bruce and Suki had become overly friendly for Louis' liking) and the association ended.

Once back home, Suki forsook the music industry to raise a family (although she and Louis later divorced). Interviewed in the mid-1980s for Backstreets, Suki mentions re-contacting Bruce to help out some local film producers, so their relationship would appear to have been cordial at this point, although she has not been accorded a full place in the official Springsteen legend, omitted as she was from the acknowledgements in *Songs* and the sleevenotes to *Greatest Hits* where other 'alumni' were listed. The inclusion of Soozie Tyrell's violin to *The Rising* tour has brought comparisons with Lahav and many have welcomed a return to a broader sound that Suki once brought E Street Band shows, however briefly.

Jon Landau

With Bruce: producer, manager. 1975–present.

Jon Landau was an established music journalist when he

joined Bruce Springsteen's team, having written for Crawdaddy! and the Rolling Stones. His forays into production were mixed, as he had a rough time working with the J. Geils Band and was then accused of taming the MC5 for their second effort, their presciently-titled *Back In The U.S.A.* album. In his regular role as reviewer, Landau made the infamous statement, "I saw rock and roll's future and its name is Bruce Springsteen" after a 1974 show and, shortly afterwards, struck up a friendship with the artist. Seeing him as a kindred spirit, Bruce called on Landau to assist in the stalled *Born To Run* sessions and the artist soon chose to sever his ties with Mike Appel, provoking the infamous legal dispute.

Outside of his work for Springsteen, Landau found time to produce three albums for Livingstone Taylor (brother of James) and Jackson Browne's 'The Pretender' (1976). Expanding his management responsibilities under the organisation Jon Landau Management, with the help of Barbara Carr (whose husband, Dave Marsh, is also a rock journalist and Bruce biographer), Natalie Merchant and Shania Twain were brought to his roster in the 1990s. After six years, during which time she had become a global superstar, Twain controversially split from him in 2002, around the time of Bruce's *The Rising*, citing Landau's preoccupation with his other major client.

In recent years, Bruce has moved away from using Landau as a producer, working with Brendan O'Brien on *The Rising*, although he remains a key figure in all Bruce activities.

Nils Lofgren (b. 21 June 1951)

With Bruce: guitar, dobro, slide guitar, banjo, vocals. 1984–89, 1995, 1999–present.

Nils Lofgren was a musical prodigy who played with a number of bar bands before he formed Grin as songwriter, guitarist and vocalist. Grin recorded four albums (for Columbia and A&M), but before the group's first album emerged, Nils was befriended by a newly solo Neil Young. Young invited the nineteen-year-old guitar maestro Lofgren to play piano (!) on the classic *After The Goldrush* (1970), while Neil guested with Grin on their debut. Nils even temporarily joined Young's backing band for their 'solo' release *Crazy Horse* (1972), while Nils' enduring friendship with Young would see him sporadically return to Young's work, appearing on the *Tonight's The Night* (1975), *Trans* (1983) and *Unplugged* (1993) albums, with Young contributing to three songs on Lofgren's 1992 effort, *Crooked Line*.

As a solo artist, Nils Lofgren enjoyed a high profile in the 1970s, recording melodic guitar-based rock ballads for A&M records, opening for acts such as the Rolling Stones and The Who and curiously writing songs with Lou Reed via the postal service. After some encouraging, if moderate, chart-placing in that decade, A&M lost interest in an act that didn't seem destined for true stardom and subsequently Nils has moved from label to label issuing some fine albums along the way and touring whenever he can. (The Grin years are well served by the 1999 Sony/Legacy release *The Very Best Of Grin*, whilst the deleted 1996 double-disc anthology *Steal Your Heart* captured the best of his 1970s solo work.)

Bruce Springsteen came calling for Nils, an occasional acquaintance, when Steve Van Zandt quit the E Street Band in 1983, but he had missed the *Born In The U.S.A.* sessions, contributing just a guest vocal to the B-side, 'Janey Don't You Lose Heart'. Indeed, 'Janey...' would be Nils' only appearance on the mammoth *Tracks* set and he was used on just two of the *Tunnel Of Love* songs.

Nils was perhaps the most excited, artistically, at the eventual 1995 and 2002 reunions of Bruce and the band, as it gave him a chance to finally record in a full E Street context. His other work has included being an integral early member of Ringo Starr's All Starr Band (alongside Clarence Clemons), writing for cinema and television, and contributing extensively to Patti Scialfa's long overdue second album, *23rd Street Lullaby*, released in 2004 (he had guested on her debut). 1995's *Damaged Goods* and 2001's *Breakaway Angel* are strong solo outings from his later career and the beautiful unplugged *Acoustic Live* is an intimate portrait of just how accomplished a guitarist Lofgren is.

Albums:
Grin, (Grin) 1971
1+1, (Grin) 1972
All Out, (Grin) 1973
Gone Crazy, (Grin) 1973
Nils Lofgren, 1975
Cry Tough, 1976
I Came To Dance, 1977
Night After Night (live), 1978
Nils, 1979
Night Fades Away, 1981

Wonderland, 1983
Flip, 1985 (the title is a reference to the former child gymnast Lofgren's – now desisted – onstage trick of playing guitar whilst bouncing on a trampoline!)
Code Of The Road (live), 1986
Silver Lining, 1991
Crooked Line, 1992
Live On The Test (live on U.K. T.V. in the 1970s), 1994
Everybreath (soundtrack), 1994
Damaged Goods, 1995
Archive Alive! (live 1985), 1997
Acoustic Live (live), 1997
New Lives (live B.B.C. radio sessions from 1980s & 1990s), 1998
Breakaway Angel, 2001
Tuff Stuff (T.V. soundtrack), 2001
The Nils Lofgren Band Live (live), 2002
Website: www.nilslofgren.com

Vini 'Mad Dog' Lopez

With Bruce: drums, background vocals. Pre-contract, 1972–1973.

A member of early Bruce bands, Lopez appeared on the first two Springsteen albums, before a combination of his perceived deficiencies as a drummer (Landau, in his job as critic had singled Lopez out as a weakness) and, sometimes violent, unpredictability saw him fired.

Lopez continued to play with various low-key Jersey Shore bands and when Bruce played in Asbury Park at the end of his 1996 *Tom Joad* tour, Lopez and other faces from the early days were called on as guests. 'Mad Dog' was also brought in to overdub some parts to the original recordings he had played on, which saw the light of day on *Tracks*.

'Southside' Johnny Lyon (And The Asbury Jukes)

With Bruce: vocals, harmonica. Pre–contract.

Johnny Lyon and Bruce Springsteen shared bandmates a–plenty in the years before Bruce signed to Columbia, finally playing alongside each other in the short-lived Dr Zoom And The Sonic Boom ensemble for which Johnny, dubbed 'Southside', blew his harmonica. Steve Van Zandt was actually missing from the early Bruce albums, helping to establish the rhythm and blues oriented Southside Johnny And The Asbury Jukes, before he claimed his E Street place as Springsteen's right-hand man. Van Zandt produced Southside's first three (and strongest) albums, released on Epic Records, and wrote the bulk of the group's material, with Bruce also contributing a number, including the classics 'The Fever' and 'Hearts Of Stone' and the debut's sleevenote. In the late 1970s, Southside Johnny was a successful act, although his band never fully broke through and a number of label changes saw their fortunes decline and sparked numerous personnel changes.

Southside has continued on, accepting his own level of success, whilst understanding that he will always be in the shadow of his Jersey contemporary. Johnny and Bruce remain friends and are still known to guest at each other's shows. Van Zandt produced a reasonably successful 1991 album, *Better Days*, on which Bruce guested, Garry Tallent took the reins for a 2002 album and Southside still regularly tours the world.

Albums:
I Don't Want To Go Home, 1976
This Time It's For Real, 1977
Hearts Of Stone, 1978
The Jukes, 1979
Sacrifice, 1980
Reach Up And Touch The Sky, 1980
Trash It Up, 1983
In The Heat, (with The Jukes) 1984
At Least We Got Shoes, (with The Jukes) 1986
Slow Dance, (solo) 1989
Better Days, 1991
Spittin' Fire, 1996
Live At The Paradise Theater, 2000
Messin' With The Blues, 2000
Going To Jukesville, 2002
Website: www.southsidejohnny.org

David Sancious

With Bruce: piano, organ, electric piano, clavinet. Pre-contract, 1972–1974, 1992.

Part of the New Jersey music scene in the late 1960s, he reportedly joined Bruce Springsteen for an onstage jam in 1970. By the following year, he was a member of the Sundance Blues Band (also featuring Steven Van Zandt and Southside Johnny) and Glory Road Band with Gary Tallent and Bill Chinnock (whose early bands would also feature Danny Federici and Vini Lopez). Sancious then became part of the large conglomeration of Jersey musicians that went by the name of Dr Zoom And The Sonic Boom. From there, he moved onto The Bruce Springsteen

Band and played on the first two albums. By 1975's *Born To Run*, however, the elongated recording sessions and David's own passion for jazz fusion prompted him to part ways with Bruce, although he had the satisfaction of playing on the legendary title track recorded the year before his departure.

Sancious next formed his own band, Tone (credited as David Sancious and Tone), with fellow E Street alumnus Ernest 'Boom' Carter, and would later include Patti Scialfa as a vocalist on *Just As I Thought*, long before her E Street Band membership. The band's first album was produced by legendary jazz drummer Billy Cobham. Tone had a checkered history, with record company run-ins resulting in two full albums being completed but unreleased during the band's lifetime.

As evidenced by his 1970s jazz work, Sancious had an unorthodox style for a rock keyboardist, but one that suited Bruce's early funk workouts. It also made Sancious an attractive prospect for more eclectic artists and post-Tone he has recorded and toured with big names, including Eric Clapton, Sting and Peter Gabriel. Touring with the latter's band during the 1988 Amnesty concerts, he was reunited professionally with Bruce. He would later rejoin his former employer on his *Human Touch* album, on various *Tracks* outtakes from the early E Street days and on into the epic sessions that evolved into Springsteen's 1992 album releases.

Albums:
Forest Of Feelings, (with Tone) 1975
Transformation (The Speed Of Love), (with Tone) 1976
Dance Of The Age Of Enlightenment, (with Tone) unreleased 1977

Tone Poems, (with Tone) unreleased 1977
True Stories, (with Tone) 1978
Just As I Thought, 1979
The Bridge, 1981
9 Piano Improvisations, 2000
Website: www.davidsancious.com

Patti Scialfa (b. 29 July 1956)

With Bruce: guitar, percussion, background vocals.
1984–present.

Nearly seven years younger than her eventual employer
and husband, Patti Scialfa grew up in a New Jersey town
not far from Bruce, with a similarly Italian and Irish
family heritage. Playing in numerous bands since her
teens, Scialfa landed early jobs on albums by ex-E Street
Band member David Sancious and Bruce's friend
Southside Johnny. Patti was recruited by Bruce for the
tour to support *Born In The U.S.A.*, and around that time
also played on *Dirty Work* by the Rolling Stones and Keith
Richards' *Talk Is Cheap*. She had landed a solo recording
deal prior to her relationship with Bruce developing on
the 1988 E Street Band world tour. The tabloids made hay
with Bruce and Patti, and Bruce's then wife Julianne
Phillips filed for divorce (although the marriage had
clearly been in difficulty for some time). Springsteen and
Scialfa's first child, Evan, was born in 1990 and the couple
were married the following year. Two more children,
Jessica Rae and Sam, were born in the next four years,
affecting the promotion of Patti's 1993 debut, *Rumble Doll*
(that featured Bruce, Roy Bittan and Nils Lofgren).

Whilst her first album had little success, it was well

regarded, and Emmylou Harris gave her support by covering 'Valerie' on her *Western Wall* project with Linda Ronstadt and inviting her to guest on *Red Dirt Girl*. Harris also played the *Rumble Doll* album over the P.A. before playing a Royal Albert Hall gig in 2000. Patti's second album, *23rd Street Lullaby*, was released in 2004 with a strong plot of television appearances and interviews, although again, it had little commercial impact.

(A portion of Patti's song 'Rumble Doll' was inserted into the regular rendition of 'Tenth Avenue Freeze-Out' during the 1999–2000 E Street band reunion world tour and was included on the *Live In New York City* album.)

Albums:
Rumble Doll, 1993
23rd Street Lullaby, 2004
Website: www.pattiscialfa.net

Garry Tallent (b. 27 October 1949)

With Bruce: bass, tuba, background vocals. Pre-contract, 1972–1989, 1995, 1999–present.

Garry Tallent was a part of the Jersey music scene as Bruce was learning his art and he played bass alongside a number of future fellow E Streeters, finally joining as part of Dr Zoom And The Sonic Boom.

Within the Springsteen family, Garry was featured on the Gary U.S. Bonds' 1980 and '81 records, helped out on Little Steven's *Men Without Women* and Danny Federici's *Flemington*, and he produced close friend Southside Johnny's 2000 album *Messin' With The Blues* for which he also co-wrote several tracks. (Garry and Southside Johnny share a large collection of rhythm and blues and rock and roll vinyl.)

As a producer and session player based in Nashville, he has attracted the admiration of the Springsteen fan and country rock maverick Steve Earle, with whom he has recorded sporadically. Other credits include Emmylou Harris, Rodney Crowell, Buddy and Julie Miller, Ian Hunter and Steve Forbert whose 1988 and 2002 albums were both produced by the bass player.

Soozie Tyrell

With Bruce: violin, background vocals. 1992, 1995, 2002–present.

Soozie Tyrell was a long-time session musician, playing with Sheryl Crow and Buster Poindexter, before Tyrell first played with Bruce. She added vocals to his 1992 *Lucky Town* and she played some memorable violin on *The Ghost Of Tom Joad* three years later, having aided her friend Patti Scialfa on her debut. Her violin greets the listener on the shimmering opening to *The Rising* and her playing and backing vocals were retained for the subsequent world tour, although she has not been granted official membership of the E Street Band in any credits as yet. In 2003, she released a solid solo album, produced by sometime Dylan band members Larry Campbell and Tony Garnier, on which Bruce and Patti guested, and Soozie was again on hand for the latter's belated second album.

Album:
White Lines, 2003
Website: www.sooizetyrell.com

Steve Van Zandt ('Miami'; 'Little Steven')
(b. 22 November 1950)

With Bruce: guitar, mandolin, vocals, arrangements and production. Pre-contract, 1975–1984, 1995, 1999–present.

Van Zandt first played with Springsteen as guitarist in Steel Mill in 1970, having been a member of the Sundance Blues Band alongside Southside Johnny and David Sancious. He swiftly became a close friend to Bruce, although he was absent from the first couple of Springsteen albums, hired as guitarist to the Dovells on the nostalgia circuit. 'Miami' Steve then concentrated on establishing another popular son of New Jersey, Southside Johnny Lyon, putting together his group, the Asbury Jukes, for whom he was primary songwriter and producer on their first three albums.

Van Zandt arrived to help arrange the horns on *Born To Run*'s 'Tenth Avenue Freeze-Out' and played the part of Bruce's buddy, to Clarence Clemons' mystical Big Man in concert until 1984. Steve had begun to produce for Bruce on *The River* and shared the credits on *Born In The U.S.A.*, but decided to leave prior to the next world tour, to pursue his own career. Having become politicised by touring so many different parts of the world with Bruce, Little Steven, a name he adopted to distinguish his musical personas, had launched his solo life with 1982's fine *Men Without Women*. He did this with a huge band dubbed the Disciples Of Soul, and this was basically a grittier take on the Southside Johnny sound he had developed (Bruce guested on this and his 1987 album). Subsequent albums were marred by worthy but plodding lyrics and some rushed production, although Van Zandt did put together the successful and influential anti-Apartheid album *Sun City* in 1985.

As a producer, aside from his Asbury Jukes work, Steve worked with Ronnie Spector, co-produced with Bruce the Gary U.S. Bonds comeback albums in the early 1980s and helped out Lone Justice. He even recorded with Bob Dylan on aborted sessions for *Empire Burlesque*, including a version of 'When The Night Comes Falling From The Sky', also featuring Roy Bittan, appearing on *The Bootleg Series Volumes 1–3*. Steve remained a good friend to Bruce after their professional split and, as Little Steven, he remixed '57 Channels (And Nothin' On)' to benefit charities in the wake of the Los Angeles riots in the early 1990s. Another New Jersey hero, Jon Bon Jovi, invited him to tour for a while, whilst Van Zandt's big break finally came when he was cast in a new television show, *The Sopranos*, a stunning show concerning the working and domestic lives of New Jersey mobsters.

A 1999 solo album featured U2's Adam Clayton, and Jason Bonham, son of the late Led Zeppelin drummer. Van Zandt had appeared at the 1995 reunion sessions and rejoined the band fully in 1999, alongside his earlier replacement, Nils Lofgren. Recently, Little Steven has championed 'Garage Rock' with a syndicated weekly radio show and hosted a series of related concerts.

Albums:
Men Without Women, (with The Disciples Of Soul) 1982
Voice Of America, 1984
Sun City, (Artists United Against Apartheid) 1985
Freedom – No Compromise, 1987
Revolution, 1989

Born Again Savage, 1999
Greatest Hits, 1999
Website: www.littlesteven.com

Max Weinberg (b. 13 April 1951)

With Bruce: drums. 1974–1989, 1995, 1999–present.

Weinberg, who had been drumming for the Broadway show *Godspell,* passed an audition to replace Ernest 'Boom' Carter in Bruce's band in 1974, during the recording of the *Born To Run* album. Through the years, Weinberg filled in periods of non-E Street activity with session work (including recording Meat Loaf's *Bat Out Of Hell* with Roy Bittan), and even wrote a book with Robert Sontelli, *Big Beat: Conversations With Rock's Greatest Drummers*. In 1990, he established his own production company/record label, Hard Ticket Entertainment, and through this produced and played on an album for the band Killer Joe that featured the rare Springsteen songs 'Club Soul City' and 'Summer On Signal Hill'.

After Bruce's decision to carry on without the E Streeters in 1989, Weinberg eventually landed the job of house band leader on U.S. television's Late Night With Conan O'Brien. Since 1993, he has led his Max Weinberg 7 on the show, with the band also featuring the horn players Richie 'La Bamba' Rosenberg, Mark Pender and Jerry Vivino, all from The Asbury Jukes and who have occasionally worked with Springsteen, most recently on *The Rising.* When the E Street Band reformed in 1999, he was given special leave of absence from his television duties and Bruce played up to Max's new job during his onstage introductions.

Album:
Max Weinberg 7, (The Max Weinberg 7) 2000

10. Bruce And The Silver Screen

Bruce may have been swift to understand that his talents were not compatible with acting, after the *Born In The U.S.A.* video shoots, but his narrative songs have attracted attention from filmmakers looking to enhance their soundtracks and, in recent years, when the project has appealed sufficiently, he has occasionally acquiesced to requests for songs. Here, in chronological order, are films to which Bruce has donated original or previously unreleased material:

Philadelphia, directed by Jonathan Demme, 1993.

Bruce contributed what turned out to be a career-revitalising song in 'Streets Of Philadelphia', a drum-machine and keyboard propelled self-examination from the point of view of someone seeing himself fading away physically and afraid to lose those around him. The song opened Demme's brave, if overly sentimental film, that saw Hollywood finally address AIDS in a major film. 'Streets Of Philadelphia' played over establishing shots of the location city, while artists such as Neil Young and Peter Gabriel also supplied powerful original songs. As a single, 'Streets Of Philadelphia' equalled Bruce's highest ever chart position (for 'Dancing In The Dark') at number two, helped by a heavily-played, low-budget video of Bruce walking through, well, streets in Philadelphia and, for his artistic satisfaction, singing a live vocal rather than lip-synching. Springsteen, who had played all the instruments on the recording, won an Oscar from his first nomination, playing at the Academy Awards ceremony with a minimal back-up band. 'Streets Of Philadelphia' also went on to pick up three Grammy Awards. Demme repaid Bruce for a song that undoubtedly enhanced his film's profile, by directing Bruce and the E Street Band's reunion performance of 'Murder Incorporated' live at Tramps in New York to promote *Greatest Hits* in 1995, and later a live video for their version of 'If I Should Fall Behind' in 2000.

The Crossing Guard, directed by Sean Penn, 1995.

In the vein of a number of mid-1990s demos (as evidenced by the releases on *Tracks*), 'Missing' is a drum-machine and keyboard-based blues song (well, it opens with the words "woke up this morning" and is about loss) and it was one of the stronger efforts he recorded during this period. Playing it to Sean Penn, the actor was impressed enough to incorporate it into the soundtrack to his Jack Nicholson-starring movie of pain and the longing for vengeance, *The Crossing Guard*. With a sound in the vein of 'Streets Of Philadelphia', an album's worth of this dark, guitar-free material would have been fascinating and certainly this is a Bruce song that deserved a wider airing at the time. 'Missing' was buried as a B-side to 'Secret Garden' on a couple of occasions in Europe, first to push *Greatest Hits*, and later when that song was itself included in a soundtrack – to Cameron Crowe's *Jerry Maguire*. 'Missing' aptly missed the cut for *Tracks*, presumably on the inconsistently adhered-to criteria that it wasn't from an official album session. The song did, however, make it to the bonus disc of *The Essential*.

Dead Man Walking, directed by Tim Robbins, 1995.

Bruce fan and friend Sean Penn took the lead role in this film by the famously left-wing Hollywood activist, Tim Robbins, playing a convicted murderer on Death Row. For a second time, Bruce was nominated for an Oscar, this time for a dark acoustic guitar-led mood piece, lyrically akin to his earlier song 'Nebraska' in which the killer does not ask for forgiveness, this time with the disturbing statement that "my sins are all I have". Powerfully the equal to 'Streets Of Philadelphia', if musically too low-key to trouble the charts, the song was amongst a great collection of original recordings on the soundtrack album (although not all were featured in the film) by the likes of Tom Waits and Mary Chapin Carpenter. This time, however, Bruce missed out on the Academy Award, although he did play at the ceremony once again, with the song failing to receive anything like the same profile as its recent predecessor. Happily, for a song that relatively few casual Bruce Springsteen fans had got to hear, it was included on *The Essential* compilation, although only on the limited edition bonus disc. (An earlier Penn effort – his directorial debut – was 1991's *The Indian Runner*. This was directly inspired by the *Nebraska* song 'Highway Patrolman', and Penn actually used his footage from his film in 2000 to construct a video for the song that appeared on the updated *Video Anthology* release.)

Limbo, directed by John Sayles, 1999.

The director of promotional videos for three of *Born In The U.S.A.*'s singles, Sayles had actually coaxed some minimal Bruce 'acting' performances for 'I'm On Fire' and 'Glory Days'. In his 1983 film *Baby, It's You*, Sayles had utilised a number of early Springsteen songs for the soundtrack that may have helped land him the Bruce job the following year. Subsequently, Bruce had wisely avoided any more acting, whilst Sayles had made intelligent and acclaimed films such as *Matewan* and *Lone Star*. *Limbo* was similarly well received if low-key and Bruce wrote a song for the film's end, and performed it in a rarely used falsetto voice. Again, this belatedly gained a wider audience when featured on the extra disc of *The Essential* album.

High Fidelity, directed by Stephen Frears, 2000.

The English director of the films *The Grifters* and *Dangerous Liaisons*, Stephen Frears made this adaptation of the highly successful Nick Hornby novel about a music-obsessed, record store-owning North London romantic failure, as a romantic comedy set in Chicago. Starring John Cusack, who co-wrote the screenplay, the film treated the essential themes of the novel sympathetically and ultimately works very satisfyingly, whilst also providing numerous opportunities for the music geek to spot their favourite albums in Cusack's flat and store. Bruce's 'The

River' is featured on the soundtrack towards the end but, most interestingly, Springsteen has a cameo – as himself – sitting astride an amp and fingering a blues riff whilst backing up Cusack's character's need to put his past relationships to rest. Many fans like to think Bruce's music speaks to them, but this film takes that a step further! (NB Nick Hornby's book of musical essays, *31 Songs*, published in the U.S. as *Songbook*, featured an impassioned piece on his love of Bruce's 'Thunder Road'. A postscript also offered up a concise defence of Springsteen against those who turned on him for his success.)

11. Official Videos And DVDs

Video Anthology 1978–2000, **directed by various, 1989, updated 2001.**

The original video release covered the period 1978–1988 and so the DVD release proved a generous updating of the package. At the pinnacle of his fame, in the mid-1980s, there were reports linking Bruce to Hollywood. Whether or not prospective producers and casting agents saw his videos and were persuaded that Bruce was no Kris Kristofferson or Cher is unclear but, happily, the world was spared Bruce expanding on his brief foray into acting, his 'talents' demonstrated by the John Sayles-directed promos for 'I'm On Fire' and 'Glory Days'. Brian De Palma, Sean Penn, Tim Robbins, Meiert Avis and Jonathan Demme were among the other directors of the thirty-three clips and performances included in the set.

In Concert: MTV UnPlugged, **Larry Jordan, 1993.**

Bruce Springsteen's shot at MTV's hugely popular Unplugged proved a huge disappointment through his decision (apparently taken very late on) to bring along his somewhat nondescript band of the time and play a full-on rock gig instead of adhering to the show's stripped acoustic premise. In addition to the (poorly packaged) album, the home video featured two tracks not shown on the original television broadcast and a total of five tracks not present on the album, while the laserdisc edition added yet another. (NB A DVD release was scheduled by Sony for late 2004.)

Blood Brothers, directed by Ernie Fritz, 1996.

Ernie Fritz was given access to the studios to follow the studio reunion of Bruce Springsteen and his long-estranged E Street Band, brought back together to record bonus material for *Greatest Hits* in 1995. There is no obvious animosity from the band to Bruce who had relinquished their services in 1989 and the atmosphere is depicted as harmonious and creative. Jon Landau is featured giving opinions on the new songs, the album artwork, tracklisting, and adding pressure to the project by issuing a statement to the press that includes a release date. Initial pressings of the home video release came with a free CD featuring material recorded during the sessions and 'Without You' remains unique to this limited edition item.

Live In New York City (recorded 29 June and 1 July 2000), directed by Chris Hilson, 2001.

This double-disc set was the first ever official release to capture the visual essence of a full Bruce Springsteen and the E Street Band concert. Taped during the final Madison Square Garden stand of the E Street Band reunion tour of

1999–2000, this set featured twenty-five songs, ranging from 'Lost In The Flood' from Bruce's debut, to the brand new 'Land Of Hope And Dreams' and 'American Skin (41 Shots)'. There was also a short documentary including interviews with Bruce and the band and featuring additional live footage. Initial pressings came with a two-song CD, featuring performances of 'My Hometown' and 'This Hard Land' recorded on the 29 June, but not included on either the album or DVD.

Live In Barcelona (recorded 16 October 2002), directed by Chris Hilson, 2003.

Another two-disc live set, coming just two years after the reunion tour release, may sound excessive, but this is a long-awaited complete single Bruce Springsteen and the E Street Band show, captured on film, and reveals a fairly typical concert structure in support of *The Rising* album. Dozens of songs were shuffled into and out of the line-up over the course of the tour, as always with Springsteen, but the twenty-four here present a strong set. As with the *Live In New York City* DVD, there is a short documentary on the tour, with extra footage.

12. Bibliography

Alterman, Eric, *It Ain't No Sin To Be Glad You're Alive: The Promise Of Bruce Springsteen*. Backbay, 2001 (updated paperback).
A political journalist, Alterman is also a big Springsteen fan. This unusual work is both a biography of Bruce, a critical analysis of some of his selected works and also an account of a fan's reaction to various career moves made by Springsteen.

Cross, Charles R. and the Editors of *Backstreets* magazine, *Backstreets: Springsteen: The Man And His Music*. New York: Harmony, 1989 (updated paperback).
This glossy tome from the team behind the Backstreets' fanzine, and now also the website, is actually illuminating. As well as pretty comprehensive detailing of every Springsteen live appearance it could get information on, and a recording career history that includes known outtakes and other details, *Backstreets* also features exclusive interviews with past and present band members, Mike Appel and Southside Johnny, and even a guide to the tourist attractions of Asbury Park.

Cullen, Jim, *Born In The U.S.A.: Bruce Springsteen And The American Tradition.* **London: Helter Skelter, 1998.**
A very readable investigation of the politics, cultural and social meaning, as well as the impact, of the music of Bruce Springsteen. Far more accessible than this description might suggest, this also acts as a history of Bruce's development into a thoughtful and responsible songwriter and musician.

Eliot, Marc with Mike Appel, *Down Thunder Road: The Making Of Bruce Springsteen.* **London: Plexus, 1992.**
This is the polar opposite of Dave Marsh's insider account of Springsteen's career, written with the 'participation' of the embittered ex-manager, Mike Appel. Eliot covers the early years with the help of Appel's reminiscences, before reaching the infamous court-case that ended Bruce's association with his manager. The appendix features eighty-five pages worth of legal documents, royalty and expense invoices, and contracts.

Gold, H.O. and Appel, M., *Follow That Dream.* **New York: Green And Pleasant, year unknown.**
Mike Appel may have sold back to Bruce any production and publishing rights he had possessed, but he was still keen enough to get some of the Bruce action to the extent that he and the mysterious H.O. Gold put together this 'bootleg' book, stating on its title page "All rights reserved, all wrongs reversed". With minimal production values, this effort collects over one hundred Bruce lyrics not readily available elsewhere, a large percentage of which remain unreleased on official recordings, even a dozen years after the 1992 close of this book.

Goodman, Fred, *The Mansion On The Hill: Dylan, Young, Geffen, Springsteen And The Head-On Collision Of Rock And Commerce*. London: Jonathan Cape, 1997.

This is a muscular and fascinating, and thoroughly compelling account, of American music giants in the 1970s. Jon Landau's experiences with the MC5, Neil Young's battles with David Geffen and the growth of Springsteen from hyped youngster to all-conquering megastar are all examined in depth.

Marsh, Dave, *Bruce Springsteen: Two Hearts: The Definitive Biography, 1972–2003*. London: Routledge, 2004.

This is a hefty volume, comprising both Marsh's original Bruce biographies, *Born To Run* and *Glory Days*, along with the introductions to various reissues of these. As the latter book took Bruce through the 1980s, the fascinating time away from the E Street Band, the mixed feelings about its reformation and eventual triumphant return should all provide plenty of material for Marsh to examine. Instead, in a book of nearly seven hundred pages, less than thirty are given over to Bruce's last five studio and two live albums, four DVD releases, four compilations of hits and rarities and several major tours. Elsewhere, the book is curiously unsatisfactory – Marsh, as husband to Bruce's assistant manager, Barbara Carr, is good at describing the progress of his friend's career, but light on criticism of Springsteen's work, or Bruce and Jon Landau's decision-making. Still, this is basically an unofficial 'official' biography and a handy work when the reader takes that into account.

The Editors of Rolling Stone, *The Rolling Stone Files.* **London: MacMillan, 1998.**
A collection of articles, interviews and contemporary news bulletins from the pages of the American music magazine.

Sandford, Christopher, *Springsteen: Point Blank.* **London: Little, Brown & Co Ltd. 1999.**
A full-blown, unauthorised biography that is more concerned with Bruce the man, and his private life, than the music.

Sawyers, June Skinner (Ed.), *Racing In The Street: The Bruce Springsteen Reader.* **Penguin (U.S.A.), 2004.**
This is a strong compilation of articles, book extracts, criticism and interviews, tracing the history of Springsteen's career chronologically. The jacket claims that the book is 'loaded with extras' in the vein of DVD packaging and, appropriately, Italian-American director Martin Scorsese provides a foreword.

Springsteen, Bruce, *Songs.* **London: Virgin, 2003 (updated paperback).**
Possibly the closest we will get to a Bruce autobiography, this project originally came out around the time of *Tracks*, obviously a period when Bruce felt content to take stock of his position before heading out once more with new material. Thus, we got a boxset of outtakes and this studio album-by-album collection of lyrics (including the first time that the words for *The Wild, The Innocent And The E Street Shuffle* were officially made available). Sandra Choron, who had previously worked as Art Director on

Bruce releases, is credited as 'Project Director' and insti-
gator of the original idea, and true to her visual sense, the
book is packed with many great photos. The real highlights, however, are Bruce's notes about the processes and
thoughts behind the albums (generally running to three or
four pages for each) and a handful of Bruce's handwritten
lyric sheets, which reveal some of his songwriting
methods, giving a glimpse of how songs evolved along the
way. An updated version appeared in 2003 and, true to
Bruce-project form, included not only the lyrics (and
notes) for *The Rising*, but also the words to *Live In New
York City*'s two exclusive tracks. The original decision to
make this a clear-cut studio album-only collection of song
lyrics, excluding B-sides, outtakes or tracks only released
on previous live releases is immediately compromised.
Granted 'Land Of Hope And Dreams' and 'American Skin
(41 Shots)' are important to present-day Bruce and are
more significant than *UnPlugged*'s 'Red Headed Woman',
but why not include 'Seeds' or 'Because The Night' as
well? Still, this is an essential acquisition for anyone interested in understanding where Bruce's music is coming
from.

13. Websites

A selection of some of the more notable of the hundreds of Springsteen-devoted internet sites.

Backstreets

As well as publishing the premier Bruce fanzine, featuring comprehensive concert setlists and interviews, the Backstreets website offers up-to-date news on Bruce and friends' appearances, recording rumours, release dates and more. It also offers "The world's best selection of Springsteen collectibles" via mail order.
www.backstreets.com

Badlands

Badlands is the online store site for the U.K. fanzine, *The Ties That Bind* (edited by the knowledgeable Jump brothers) – subscription to this gives access to a wealth of long-deleted and hard-to-find releases and is essential for a Bruce fan! The publication carries Bruce reports, setlists and forthcoming releases in its occasional glossy issues, with regular supplements supplying up-to-date news. Badlands arranges trips across the world to see Bruce whenever he tours and these are available to book on the

website, which also features Bruce merchandise for sale, along with other like-minded artists.
www.badlands.co.uk

The Boots

The news is not updated as regularly here as on rival sites and is often second-hand, but it does feature an excellent setlist section running from the start of the 1999 E Street Band reunion tour to the present.
www.theboots.net

Bruce Base

For those who like their information in huge depth, this website provides listings of EVERY known Bruce gig. Perhaps of particular interest are the early years, prior to Springsteen's recording contract, where Bruce's appearances in bands such as Steel Mill are included. Concert setlists (where available – and that's impressively often), guest appearances, photos, ticket scans and details of any bootlegs of each show are given. An amazing extra feature for some listings is a link to the song introductions (that make Bruce concerts more than just performer and audience, bringing the two closer together by adding context and often humour and warmth) – look for the Storyteller signs. When you're at a Bruce concert, these rambles are great fun, but it's a little worrying that fans find the time to carefully transcribe them!
www.brucebase.shetland.co.uk

Bruce Springsteen – Official Site

Revamped in 2003, Sony's official Bruce site – as with so many label-backed pages – fails to deliver. In the summer of 2004, the front news page carried details of buying tickets for 'newly' added concerts that had actually taken place eight months previously. Whilst it would not be expected to carry the minutiae that more obsessive fans will keep each other posted of, the clearly out-of-date information for such an important artist is extremely lazy and disappointing. Doubtless it will snap into action when next there is an official piece of merchandise to sell.

From the menu page, as well as the prerequisite merchandise link (to Sony Music Store), there is a song index from which the lyrics to any Bruce song released on an official album can be located. Curiously, the site compilers have incorporated the live covers Bruce has officially released into the index and, whilst the correct writing credits are given and lyrics unsurprisingly not included, Springsteen is listed as the copyright holder. Bruce may no longer be as naïve as when he first signed with Mike Appel, but Tom Waits is unlikely to have given away his rights to 'Jersey Girl', even if Bruce did tweak the lyrics! The B-sides that didn't make the cut for *Tracks* are also irritatingly missing from this site.
www.brucespringsteen.net

Greasy Lake

This is a well-constructed site, with countless sub-menus to articles, setlists and Bruce trivia. It doesn't carry much in the way of current news, but does have links to a

number of alternative Bruce sites and also includes links for related artists and even present-day musicians on the Jersey scene.
www.greasylake.org

Killing Floor

An amazingly detailed and well-organised site – it refers to itself as "the Bruce Springsteen Database". Lyrics to just about every song Bruce has ever performed are available, as are details of where and when.
www.brucespringsteen.it